LASTGASPISM

LASTGASPISM:
Art and Survival in the Age of Pandemic

By
Anthony Romero
Daniel Tucker
Dan S. Wang

With
Kimberly Bain
Sandra de la Loza
Cheryl Derricotte
Design Studio for Social Intervention
Erin Genia
Pato Hebert
Damon Locks
Kelli Morgan
Karthik Pandian

Soberscove Press | Chicago

CONTENTS

LASTGASPISM: *An Introduction*

Anthony Romero, Daniel Tucker, and Dan S. Wang

In 2020, COVID-19, a readily transmitted airborne coronavirus against which the human species bears no accumulated immunity, commandeered the human narrative and ushered in the global pandemic that public health experts had long feared. As of this writing, eighteen months into the pandemic, the virus has killed 4.5 million people worldwide, including approximately 640,000 persons in the US, statistical snapshots destined to be notable only for the smallness of the figures in relation to whatever the count stands at any future point.[1] The early surges of the virus were helped along by "superspreader" events and other exponential infection scenarios, forcing quarantines, lockdowns, and massive disruptions to everyday life. The vibrant street life of cities descended into a surreal pall of suspended time and indoor isolation as localized infection hotspots erupted in every part of the country, both urban and rural, in staggered waves as the year unfolded. On a micro level, members of a household often successively caught the virus, in turn suffering bouts of fevered breathing and the dreaded dry cough—with the worst stricken forced onto ventilator-assisted breathing—or expressing no symptoms at all, such unevenness being

[1]
World Health Organization, Coronavirus Dashboard, accessed September 5, 2021, https://covid19.who.int/.

the cunning of the virus. By the summer of 2021, aka
Pandemic Year Two, a new layer of complexity defined
the US situation. The advent of effective and well-
distributed vaccines blunted the spread for several months.
However, the quasi-respite ended with the arrival of the
ultra-infectious Delta variant, which, in combination with
regionally concentrated vaccine hesitancy, produced
new waves of hospitalization. The road to endemicity
promises to be bumpy.

While pandemic fatigue undoubtedly includes
the tiresome need to think and talk about it, our
commitment is to consider the pandemic as an event
that has reframed and catalyzed numerous other crises
and possible resolutions. This is a particular quality
of it that is difficult to articulate: on the one hand, the
pandemic imposed a swift reordering of daily life,
altering how we work and how we care for ourselves,
our children, and our loved ones. The effects of this
reorientation have reverberated out from the personal
and include major adjustments on the part of schools,
the government, and corporations as well, often to the
detriment of household economic security. And, on the
other hand, the pandemic has given issues of inequality
greater visibility than they have had in generations. A
year and a half since the first lockdowns were put into
place, COVID and inequality are nearly inseparable insofar
as the global pandemic continues to evolve, exposing
the staggering resource and access gaps among us.

Compounding Crisis

While COVID was the common denominator and the
invisible threat, the quickened pace of other events
throughout 2020 also left many gasping for air. With
health experts responding to an unfolding public
health calamity of historic proportions while being undermined at every turn by a science-ignorant US president,
each strange new development ratcheted up the anxiety
meter. The hyperinertia of quarantine rendered the

stimuli of tweet streams and social media feeds more breathless than usual. And even without the actual contraction of the coronavirus disease, crowded living spaces and excessive screen time cramped domestic airspace as work and school went virtual.

As afflicted bodies struggled with oxygen levels—noted early on as mostly male and mostly older,[2] in a poetically biopolitical twist—a US election season transpired that included some of the oldest presidential candidates in history.[3] This evidence of gerontocracy exacerbated tensions over generational leadership transitions, whether in workplaces or on the political stage, while, simultaneously, there was widespread grief around losing community elders.

Following the circulation of a video documenting the murder of George Floyd by a white Minneapolis police officer in May 2020, spontaneous protest and revolt energized longstanding organizing around police brutality and racial justice. In cities across the US, demonstrations and direct action produced a plethora of responses, advancing calls ranging from accountability to abolition. Building on years of viral content and chants of "Say her name" and "Say his name," rallies responding to police violence featured placards with the names of past victims of police violence. "I can't breathe" reappeared as an anguished rallying cry among the millions demonstrating across the country, echoing the words of a gasping Eric Garner as he was choked to death by another white police officer in New York City in 2014.

Not to be contained by a single issue, the declaration "I will breathe" was expanded beyond its initial use and painted on the street in Philadelphia outside an encampment that channeled the energy of the protests for racial justice into a demand for housing. Given the concurrent pressures of racial profiling, threats of eviction, and pandemic-induced mass unemployment, breath and breathing as slogan touchpoints indicated the merged crises, particularly in terms of their disproportionate impact on Black people. The stacked events of pandemic hotspots and extrajudicial killings of

2
Research and statistical analysis of populations and patient profiles have been part of the story of COVID-19 from the beginning; never has a disease had this level of both epidemiological and clinical attention at once, worldwide. The apparent difference in COVID fatality rates of older people and men emerged as an early pandemic observation, along with higher case rates among women (but lower fatality rates). The statistical dimorphism has since been shown as measurable in studies of various contexts and with various intent. For example, this study based on national data collection of the People's Republic of China concludes that men of virtually all age groups suffer significantly higher rates of critical cases and case fatality. J. Qian, L. Zhao, R. Z. Ye, X. J. Li, and Y. L. Liu "Age-Dependent Gender Differences in COVID-19 in Mainland China: Comparative Study, *Clinical Infectious Diseases: An Official Publication of the Infectious Diseases Society of America* 71, no. 9 (2020): 2488–94, https://doi.org/10.1093/cid/ciaa683. As an example of a study of different intent, in pursuing a question about comorbidities, this study of a New York City population uncovers similar age and gender correlations with higher mortality rates: E. Klang, S. Soffer, G. Nadkarni et al., "Sex Differences in Age and Comorbidities for COVID-19 Mortality in Urban New York City," *SN Comprehensive Clinical Medicine* 2 (2020): 1319–22, https://doi.org/10.1007/s42399-020-00430-w. Most departments of public

health in the US provide publicly available COVID statistics. Demographic data broken down by age and gender consistently document comparatively higher absolute numbers of male deaths. Age group deaths have shifted since older groups have been vaccinated at higher rates than younger groups. For example, data from the state of Michigan, "Coronavirus/Michigan Data," Michigan.gov, accessed September 28, 2021, https://www.michigan.gov/coronavirus/0,9753,7-406-98163_98173---,00.html.

3
Paige Winfield Cunningham, "The Health 202: President Trump and Joe Biden Are the Oldest Nominees for President, Ever," *Washington Post*, August 17, 2020, https://www.washingtonpost.com/politics/2020/08/17/health-202-president-trump-joe-biden-are-oldest-nominees-president-ever/.

4
Jeffrey Gettleman, "India Savors a Rare Upside to Coronavirus: Clean Air," *New York Times*, April 8, 2020, https://www.nytimes.com/2020/04/08/world/asia/india-pollution-coronavirus.html.

5
"Air Pollution Is Returning to Pre-COVID Levels," *The Economist*, September 5, 2020, https://www.economist.com/graphic-detail/2020/09/05/air-pollution-is-returning-to-pre-covid-levels.

Black people revealed a "syndemic" in which COVID risk factors, such as hypertension and obesity, are bundled up in populations suffering from the structural racism of inaccessible healthcare, overpolicing, and mass incarceration.

COVID-19 lockdowns instituted in the early days of the pandemic, from March to June 2020, had, among other effects, that of allowing for urban ecological exhalations; this was noted in cities around the world. Residents of Beijing, a megacity notorious for months-long stretches of ochre-tinged, choke-inducing air, enjoyed air with no taste. Los Angeles seemed other-worldly without its usual twelve-hour-a-day gridlocked traffic. And Delhi's dangerously high measurements of small-particulate pollution plummeted and stayed low for a couple of months; some locals claimed that stars were visible at night for the first time in more than two decades.[4] In a pandemic stingy with silver linings, these kinds of unexpectedly quick reversals of environmental fortune had city dwellers literally breathing easier.

The welcome urban atmospheric clearance proved temporary. As lockdowns were lifted, upticks in pollution-producing activity took hold nearly everywhere by the end of 2020, even as many parts of the world suffered through winter surges of infection and death.[5] That the lockdown restrictions could have such an immediate and visible effect on the air we breathe became one more suspect observation regarding the cumulative effect of industrial activity. It can be no coincidence that air travel is both the worst per capita carbon-producing human activity and the quickest way for pathogens to jump borders.

Beginning in August and continuing through to Election Day in November 2020, climate chaos wreaked havoc in the United States, no longer as an exception but rather a new and horrible norm. In Oregon, where more than a million acres of forest burned in 2020, residents up and down the Willamette Valley sealed their windows and filtered their indoor air. The fires of Northern California produced a days-long "airpocalypse"

LASTGASPISM: AN INTRODUCTION

of cinnabar skies, magnifying the psychological vise of San Francisco's lockdown, one of the earliest and strictest in the country. Like COVID, the acute wildfire crisis presented at once a large-scale event affecting millions *and* a threat to each individual's health and safety, with airborne threat the bottom line in both. Not to be outdone, the 2020 Atlantic hurricane season tallied thirty named storms, the most on record for a single season. The extreme fires and storms of 2021 that hit many parts of the world continued this trend.

Human-exacerbated "natural" disasters shared headlines with an incumbent administration that ushered COVID-19 directly into the West Wing, such that many of us spent much of the fall holding our collective breath. Election Day offered no reason to release it: Donald Trump's attempts to overturn the presidential election generated yet another crisis in the first year of the pandemic, which eventually reached fever pitch with the Capitol assault on January 6, 2021. The episode may have gained steam over Trump's lame-duck weeks, but the anxiety fueling the would-be shock troop putsch was triggered much earlier. Key moments tell the tale: white supremacists marching in Charlottesville in 2017 to the chant of "You will not replace us"; the Trump administration's sustained effort to sabotage the 2020 census; the president's call during a nationally televised debate for extremists to "stand back and stand by."[6] The fear of declining white dominance was directly tied to pro-Trump support when journalists conclusively mapped the correlation between Capitol insurrectionists and the changing racial demographics of their home counties.[7] According to the descriptions of some of the insurrectionists themselves, the invasion of the Capitol was a last stand of sorts.

From "Last Gasp" to Lastgaspism

The figure of speech "last gasp" is frequently encountered in news media headlines that attempt to articulate the

6
"Proud Boys Celebrate after Trump's Debate Callout," NBC News, September 30, 2020, https://www.nbcnews.com/tech/tech-news/proud-boys-celebrate-after-trump-s-debate-call-out-n1241512.

7
"Fears of White People Losing Out Permeate Capitol Rioters' Towns, Study Finds," *New York Times*, April 6, 2021, https://www.nytimes.com/2021/04/06/us/politics/capitol-riot-study.html.

8
German Lopez, "Sha'Carri Richardson and the Last Gasp of the War on Marijuana," (headline since modified), July 7, 2021, https://www.vox.com/22565419/shacarri-richardson-olympics-marijuana-ban-war-on-drugs.

9
Louisa Lim, "Hong Kong's Last Gasp," *New York Times*, June 29, 2021, https://www.nytimes.com/2021/06/29/opinion/hong-kong-apple-daily.html.

10
Mijente (@ConMijente), Twitter, January 26, 2021, 8:34 p.m., https://twitter.com/ConMijente/status/135424136955 2924672?s=20.

late phase of some sociopolitical struggle or the dying fashionability of once-popular values. Recent examples include the controversy over Sha'carri Richardson's exclusion from the 2021 Tokyo Olympics, described by a *Vox* news headline as the "The Last Gasp of the War on Marijuana."[8] Or a June 2021 *New York Times* op-ed about the struggle over freedom of the press in Hong Kong that ran under the headline "Hong Kong's Last Gasp."[9] This rhetoric, which typically conjures in the imagination something like a dying breath or deathbed scene, would suggest that a war, a city, conflict, policy, social struggle, or ideology is nearing its end, but it takes only a few minutes of reading to know that this is not wholly true. The War on Cannabis, now a century old and a precursor to the wider War on Drugs, is of course not over. Nor, for that matter, is Hong Kong. The intended meanings behind the rhetorical use of "last gasp" are slippery by design. Its use alerts us to a foreseen end, not the end itself. Rather, the phrase prepares us for the next phase of a conflict, the onset of closing moments, however long those moments may last. Like the pause between anxious breaths, it announces the final act of a social, cultural, or political drama. When the curtain will finally fall, however, is anybody's guess.

Between November 2020 and January 2021, *The Hill, The Nation, Vanity Fair, New York Magazine*, and *Bloomberg News* all ran stories with headlines that heralded the "last gasp" of Donald Trump's presidency; it was likewise in the Twitterverse of social media commentary. Even after Trump was out of office, the Latinx organization Mijente offered followers a good example of this rhetorical turn in January 2021, when it tweeted its condemnation of a Texas judge who blocked President Biden's one hundred–day moratorium on deportations. The tweet read, "W/ the #Texas block of @POTUS' 100 day moratorium on deportations, the attacks on our wins are already happening. This WILL be remembered as one of the last gasps of the Trump administration's racist, xenophobic legacy."[10]

LASTGASPISM: AN INTRODUCTION

This stream of headlines and tweets not only signaled the end of the Trump presidency but encouraged us to remain attentive witnesses to its final phases and aftereffects. As Trump resisted all transitional work during his lame-duck term, it became clear that his grip on American democracy was, in fact, nowhere near at an end. If anything, when Trump incited an attempted coup at the Capitol on January 6, 2021, we saw that his presidency was fundamentally based upon the continuation of a very old strain of American racism, reignited and reorganized for the twenty-first century. The final spasms of his presidency were an expression of his amalgamated chauvinism, a combined stew of nationalism, white supremacy, and misogyny. January 6 was a desperate effort to reassert those ruling privileges.

As we prepared this book, part of what we wrestled with was not only the rhetorical dimensions of "last gasp," but also the frequency of its use. It makes perfect sense that as the world grapples with an uncontrollable airborne virus, respiratory metaphors would proliferate in the media. Thus, we can see the frequency of "last gasp" in part as a byproduct of our collective preoccupation with breath and breathing, a concern exemplified by some of the contributions to this book. But the proliferation of the phrase tells us more. There are other truths buried beneath the headlines and compounding crises. The inventory of events that we have laid out, as dramatic and unfinished as they are, could also be taken as a litany of symptoms—ruptures resulting from tectonic shifts that have been building tension for decades and even centuries, tensions that the repeated "last gasps" signal. The many appearances of "last gasp" in the popular media bear witness to a larger turn of world historical dimensions: the terminal crisis of capitalism, dramatic generational transitions, a prolonged erosion of climate stability, the depletion of resources necessary for the basic sustenance of life and the inability of nation-states—and liberal democracies in particular—to manage pressures at a planetary scale. The developments of 2020–21 presage the end of the stage of gradual change, with intervals between gasps shortening. Here is where we turn from "last gasp" as proclaiming the inflection point on a given issue to Lastgaspism as a general phenomenon, a context unbounded by any particular struggle, and instead a holistically urgent framework for the aesthetics and strategies of social engagement of all kinds.

Our synthetic term Lastgaspism is an "ism" of a phenomenological rather than an ideological nature that helps us make sense of the interlocked, variably scaled crises of the unfolding present. As we write this introduction, nine months into year two of the pandemic, it is the "last" in Lastgaspism that begs consideration more than the "gasp." Last implies a duration, and last also entails a first. This is an issue of periodicity, of what constitutes periods of time and, even more importantly, the transitional measure in between periods.

Lastgaspism is not only about the struggle of the gasp, but what that struggle means as both the ending of a period as well as a struggle with a new beginning to follow. In advancing this term, this idea, this condition of Lastgaspism, we profess not only the dire predictions of what has become a commonplace eschatology, but also the affirmations of *what's next*.

Breathing Together

As for the genesis of this book, it evolved out of conversations between the three of us that began during the first lockdown. As artists and frequent collaborators, we leaned on each other to interpret what we were experiencing. Having previously processed contemporary social conditions together through the dual lenses of art and activism—in the publications *The Social Practice that Is Race* and *Organize Your Own*, which began as an exhibition and an event series—it felt natural to develop another collaborative inquiry into the present age of the pandemic.[11] For the purposes of interpreting a common political landscape, this project largely focuses on the

11
Anthony Romero and Dan S. Wang, *The Social Practice that Is Race* (Minneapolis: Beyond Repair, 2016); Anthony Romero, ed., *Organize Your Own: The Politics and Poetics of Self-Determination Movements* (Chicago: Soberscove Press, 2016). Daniel Tucker curated the exhibition on which the book was based, and Dan S. Wang was one of the many artists featured.

United States, though the compounding and expanding challenges of the present moment are hardly constrained by national borders; the pandemic is, after all, a global phenomenon.

Though we assembled it during the first two years of a pandemic, this book is not exactly a chronicle of art in pandemic times. A project truly contemporary to the period of its making is conceived, evolves, and bears fruit, all in a contingent unfolding. Occupying space between art criticism (as the first draft) and art history (as the ostensibly conclusive word) and moving across a wide spectrum of "art speak" and social movement culture, this book contains interviews, essays, artist portfolios, and experimental writings. Together, the contributions represent a range of approaches to survival and sense-making in a moment of considerable bewilderment. Along with the contributing artists and critics, we are trying to make sense of this time by documenting, reflecting on, and giving shape to the painful emergence of a new world out of the brittle shell of the old, as this emergence takes place at home; amid protests; and in the spaces of parks, museums, and prisons. It is the beginning of a new world that, like COVID, is upon us, ready or not. *Lastgaspism: Art and Survival in the Age of Pandemic* is our attempt at articulating the ends buried beneath the intersecting systems, practices, and crises that define the present moment.

Absent an ideological frame adequate to addressing the overwhelming complexity of our current predicament, aesthetic and spiritual dimensions return as zones in which to find direction and orientation. The cries of fake news and the rampant irrationality of conspiracy thinking, fueled by the ambiguous origins of COVID-19 and amplified by the deliberate sowers of confusion, are phenomena indicating a failed consensus. Rebuilding this consensus will not happen through the primacy of information and knowledge. Redefining a social consensus requires the rediscovery of a collective purpose and, in order for that to happen, we need more than data. Our editorial/curatorial process has included some of that constructive reimagination, an effect of the pandemic months we three spent in chosen kinship and study, discussing and working through the concept of Lastgaspism as conditions changed from week to week. This book is obviously not an exhaustive articulation of our thoughts on the matter; rather, it presents a collection of responses by cultural workers made in dialogue and collected with care. These are aesthetic and spiritual signposts, produced in our networks by committed artists and writers, individuals and groups doing the hard work of *feeling* their way through the worlds that are ending. Our collaboration expanded when we invited others into the process, and this now includes you. What you hold in your hands is a device for collaborative comprehension of the present and a passageway into a future in which we can all breathe easier.

EXHALING PEACE:
An Interview with Sandra de la Loza

Dan S. Wang

I was introduced to Sandra de la Loza by the artist
Nicolas Lampert in 2013. Lampert had invited her to the
University of Wisconsin–Milwaukee as a visiting artist
and insisted that I join him for her public lecture. I was
taken by the depth of her engagement and by her many
projects that excavate the hidden histories of struggle
and cultural survival in and around present-day Los
Angeles, a city largely unknown to me but for its popular
image. She seemed to work from a place of multiple
commitments and organized projects that moved easily
between historical research and popular education
to poetic treatments of archival documents, all shaded
with the directness and sophistication of conceptual art.
Her projects take viewers and participants backward in
time but also set up conditions for speculations on and
longings for a brighter, more humane future. They bring
bodies into both uniquely fashioned temporary indoor
spaces and historically loaded outdoor locations. When
I arrived in Los Angeles some years later, de la Loza was

one of the artists who initiated a very appreciated welcome and offered me invaluable local intelligence. That's when I learned about her meditation practice, which only deepened my interest in her story of personal and artistic evolution. We spoke by Zoom in January 2021, when we were just across town from one another, as the COVID-19 surge hit a macabre peak in Los Angeles with ambulance sirens heard at all hours of the day.

Dan S. Wang (DW): All right, recording now. Let me begin with a land acknowledgment. We are speaking to each other from our homes, which means that both of us are sitting within the confines of present-day Los Angeles, a settlement built on unceded lands originally and continuously inhabited by the Tongva and other Indigenous peoples.

It's important for people like myself, descended from relative latecomers to this continent, to put our own presence into the context of settlement. It also serves as a jumping-off point to have you talk about your relationship to this place and all its layered histories. Much of your work is about exploring the details of those various layers. It's intriguing to me, but how about in your own words?

Sandra de la Loza (SL): Thank you for inviting me into this conversation. Yes, I'm in Highland Park in north-eastern Los Angeles, adjacent to the neighborhood that I grew up in, El Sereno, where my parents moved in the early 1960s. My father still resides there. He is ninety-one years old.

They arrived there when they were displaced by the building of the I-5 freeway in the late '50s. My parents were born and raised here in Los Angeles. They came of age during World War II, and they were zoot suiters—they were Pachucos. They're part of that subculture. Their parents had migrated from New Mexico on my mother's side, and from northern Mexico on my father's side.

I have a great-great-grandmother on my dad's side who was born in the San Gabriel Mission. I just learned about her. There is a lot of silence around my dad's mother's history because he never really knew her. She died of an illegal abortion when he was eighteen months old. I actually don't know how far back my roots in this land go. That's a line of investigation I hope to have the honor of exploring sometime.

Lately, that space of unknowing has been important in my practice, but also in my larger inquiries, as an urban mestiza from the Indigenous diaspora and also as an artist who does a lot of research-based work and thinks about, enters, and collects archives and is aware of all the problematics that are rife in the archive. This space of not knowing and of unknowing has been a fertile space—a space of entry, of starting points.

DW: It's interesting. I'm just thinking of my family: it's very diasporic in the sense of wandering, crossing oceans, and having a peripatetic, generational narrative going back a couple of generations through different countries. Whereas in your case, you have the Chicano thing of having boundaries and geographical identities imposed on peoples who may not be moving far, if at all.

Also, I'm thinking about your projects, which sometimes have very specific sites and spaces depicted or identified, having all of these different points in these various histories, social and personal, but then having all of these blank spots or gaps. That speaks to some of the questions that I have for you.

SL: I understand my work as building a relationship with this land, and it's one of the things I've dedicated my life to. Inevitably, that means diving into history. One thing the work has taught me is that these gaps, these absences, are always surfacing in unpredictable, unexplained, and unanticipated ways.

That's one thing that also resonates with mindfulness practice: the richness of the silence. It is listening deeply to this land, deeply to the research practices, listening deeply to myself, and allowing things to surface.

DW: Can you recall for us what your early exposures to Buddhism, Buddhist practices, and Buddhist concepts were? At what point did you adopt these practices in your own life? In your early practice, was there something that was surprising or difficult, or immediately beneficial?

SL: Yes, please feel free to ask follow-up questions to help me flesh it out, because there are a lot of threads that come together in those questions.

Where was I introduced to Buddhism? I think I'm more aware of the context. The context was around 2008, when I was installing an exhibit for my first major museum show. It was at LACMA and the show was called *Phantom Sightings: Art after the Chicano Movement.*

A couple of weeks before, I had received a call from my brother, who told me that my mother had cancer. I remember the exhibition opening as such a bizarre experience. I describe it like the dream that many of us have had where you're in a very public space, completely naked, just very raw and vulnerable. That's what the opening felt like to me. One of my most public moments was also one of my most vulnerable moments. She went into a major operation like two days after the opening. We didn't know if she was going to make it. She did, but then she passed away a couple of years later. This personal context coincides with the context of the housing market beginning to bounce back after the subprime mortgage crisis. I was very aware of larger shifts happening in Los Angeles, seeing the surge of momentum we call gentrification tangibly changing the worlds that I knew.

I'd seen gentrification in other places, like in the Bay Area, where I went for undergrad at Berkeley. I had friends living in the Mission when gentrification processes happened in San Francisco ten years earlier. I saw the relentless pace that urban capitalist redevelopment had on those neighborhoods. I saw it happening in LA. Everything that I knew and loved, the neighborhoods I had dedicated my life to, that shaped me, were being

EXHALING PEACE

impacted by processes of displacement. I also felt myself vulnerable as an adjunct professor, as an artist. I was feeling my own and my family's precarity. I was in a place where nothing was stable; there was no solid ground.

I was floundering, figuring out how and where to proceed. This time really turned everything inside out and made me question my art practice, my relationships, my means of making a living, whether I could even afford to continue living in Los Angeles. Everything seemed unstable.

DW: This convergence of upheavals began around 2008?

SL: Yes. I knew something had to shift. I'm going to go on tangents because there is a lot here. In terms of art institutions, I also was becoming very disillusioned. In my art practice I wasn't having the conversations or finding the communities or the folks who were questioning the institutions we were entering. I was very conflicted about that. I didn't feel like I had support for what I was going through. I took a step back and began rooting myself in the communities that I came up in.

I went to college basically as crack hit LA in the late '80s. My generation was hugely impacted. My family was impacted. I came back three weeks after the 1992 riots and then spent pretty much the next decade in youth-run, autonomous, collectively structured spaces. That organizing created other spaces in very difficult times.

I returned to that and began doing anti-gentrification work. I also became involved in an amazing project by a great friend and someone I can consider a mentor, Olivia Chumacero, called Everything Is Medicine, around 2010. She was care-taking a native garden near Chinatown. It was a project started by Lauren Bon called Not a Cornfield, but through her participation, Olivia began Everything Is Medicine. She created space for a large body of volunteers to care for native plants. Through her workshops, events, and work sessions, we began to cultivate a relationship to the land. She also invited in Tongvan cultural bearers to share their knowledge, introduce the uses of plants, and share their histories. That is where I began to feel regrounded. My activism, cultural work, and art organizing were seminal for me in terms of helping me to move through difficult times and address the large-scale sociopolitical and economic violence and the spiritual violence that was impacting both me personally and the communities that I lived in.

But, still, my own familial trauma—what was going down with my family—was present and lingering. I was carrying a lot of pain—ghosts—for a long time. For example, I went to Berkeley in '86 as a first-generation college student. I come from a community in which our high schools have like 50 percent dropout rates. So I'm a rarity as someone who had that opportunity. The day I took my SAT, which was a gateway to Berkeley, I came home to the news that my oldest brother had ODed. Soon after I went to Berkeley, another brother lost his footing to crack, and he struggled with that for over twenty years. I am happy to share that he spent his last few years alive sober.

I began to explore different modalities, for lack of a better word, to do some self-care and healing. In the early '90s I was introduced to Indigenous ceremonies. As my mom was crossing, a series of sweat-lodge ceremonies were super important for me. But I wasn't finding the structure to hold a sustained practice in relationship to Indigenous ceremonies. I was trying lots of healing practices here and there to deal with my inner turmoil and to find tools to heal myself through a lot of experimentation. I joined various women-of-color, feminist, and decolonial support circles and organized around raw and ancestral foods, talking circles, acupuncture, Everything Is Medicine, full-moon ceremonies, you name it. All were helpful.

I got connected to an emerging sphere of politicized queer and women of color, healers. Social media was just starting to come into prominence. I got

EXHALING PEACE

introduced to Thích Nhất Hạnh around this time, and I began reading his books. I was grappling with how to bring my political work, my outward activist work, into alignment with this internal work.

DW: Let me just note the political link here. Subcultures of political engagement and grassroots activism in my experience—and, generationally speaking, we are the same—through the '80s and '90s for sure, often burned people out. Sometimes those worlds were not helpful in settling one's internal turmoil, as you say.

SL: Yes, exactly. In those circles and spaces, there wasn't a lot of acknowledgment or understanding that social transformation can be both outward and inward. And that the process of change is social but it's also personal. Maybe we need to be active on all those fronts.

It was very alive for me, obviously, with what I just shared about what was going on with me at that point. You know bell hooks and Cherríe Moraga, women-of-color writers who were combining the personal and the social. But Thích Nhất Hạnh's writings were important because they offer practical guidance for dealing with internal worlds and emotions, and for dealing with pain as part of a larger political praxis. He was also a monk who spoke about capitalism, legacies of colonization, and war. It wasn't depoliticized.

Long story short, I've been practicing yoga for ten or fifteen years, and that helped me to process my pain and go inward, but maybe not consciously. It was more of a body-based work, and at that time yoga spaces in LA were very white and New Agey. For ten years, often I would be one of only a couple Latinas in classes of sixty people. It was very, very white. Then I heard about a POC meditation retreat at Deer Park, which is a monastery in Escondido just outside of San Diego that was founded by Thích Nhất Hạnh. I signed up.

It was a beautiful retreat. A lot of the healing practices that had helped me came together in a powerful, solid alignment at that retreat. I felt, for the first time, that there was actually a structure that housed practices that could help me cultivate a transformative inner alignment. It resonated deeply with me. I wanted to learn more. That is what introduced me to Buddhist practices. Deer Park is really special because it is run by the monks, so we were practicing alongside monastics. Yes, that is what brought me in.

DW: Around when was that?

SL: Maybe 2013.

DW: There are a lot of reasons to appreciate Thích Nhất Hạnh. For example, the "everydayness" of his approach. As you say, making concrete the concepts and practices in relation to what we live. He's one of the people that talks about *samsara*, the wheel of suffering, which in human experience manifests itself in generational cycles. That is the wheel right there. It is not abstract.

Since you mentioned the retreat, could you break down the nitty-gritty of the practice? As in your introduction to a sitting practice, the focus on breathing and grounding one's mind in one's breath, do you recall that being particularly illuminating? How about in relation to aspects of your creative life, of your political life? What kinds of significance emerged in terms of the breathing?

SL: So much! Where do I start? One of the core practices of Insight meditation, one of the core Buddhist practices, is a focus on the breath. I've learned so much from it. I'd say one of the big lessons, and a big shift for me, was learning to drop my consciousness from my mind down into the body.

The Enlightenment's privileging of the mind has driven colonization and impacted the shape and textures of colonization. I think one of the huge legacies of colonization, as someone who comes from lineages of the colonized here in the Americas, is the disconnection from other knowledges. Learning to breathe helped me to listen to my body and to realize how noisy the mind is.

It's helped me become aware of narratives in my mind that disconnect me from embodied or intuitive knowledge, ancestral knowledge, knowledges of the Earth, the knowledges of deep listening—to myself, to others, and also to the Earth. Yes, there's so much there. (*Chuckles.*)

DW: That's why it makes sense as a gift, because, as you say, the breath can provide a kind of access to suppressed thinking or parts of one's existence that are less touched by colonialism. It is available; that's the miracle of it.

Let me ask about the social dimensions of a mindfulness practice. In the last ten or fifteen years, there's been a growth in self-identified people of color and LGBTQI people adopting such practices and finding sangha. The teacher Larry Yang graphed out the estimated numbers of self-identified BIPOC practitioners, and there's an exponential upward curve starting around 2010.

How do you see what's happening in this landscape of practice in the United States? You alluded to it regarding the first retreat that you attended. What do you make of these trends?

SL: That first retreat led to others. So far, I've only attended POC retreats. From these I was introduced to Spirit Rock and the East Bay Meditation Center, which was cofounded by Larry Yang. I was attracted to this growing sphere of people-of-color practitioners who were practicing with an understanding that Buddhist practices can be helpful tools in terms of moving toward liberation that is outwardly political and works toward social change but is also an inward pathway to grapple with ancestral trauma and historic violence. These practices are vital for evolving ways of working toward decolonizing, both socially and individually.

I've mostly sat in POC sanghas. I established my own sangha with some friends here in northeast Los Angeles, which is still active. I'm about to begin my first foray into a more mainstream mindfulness practice for my own growth. This is a two-year training program.

DW: Is that an Insight meditation-affiliated thing?

SL: It's through Jack Kornfield, founder of Spirit Rock, and Tara Brach. Two white practitioners. I'm grateful to have had years in primarily POC-led sangha spaces. I feel ready to enter a more mainstream space.

DW: You talked a little bit about healing and historical traumas. Do you see Buddhist practices as a part of the liberation work that needs to be done?

SL: I think there are practical tools that can really help activist spaces. In my adult life, I've moved between activist work to my personal artistic practice. From art circles to community-based organizing circles, back and forth, and sometimes in both at once. There are various reasons why I didn't become a full-time activist—I mean, how do you afford to become a full-time organizer? That was just one of the struggles. The other relates to toxicity within social justice efforts; having some experiences in which worthwhile social justice efforts and spaces implode has also kept me moving. Then there are my struggles with the possibility of art, and my own disillusionment with the institutions and cultures within art and art circuits. I'm always going back and forth.

I do believe these practices can help us. I see this in myself. As I'm growing a mindfulness practice, it has helped me to not react so quickly. It has helped me to stop and listen. Organizing around issues like gentrification, the intensity of organizing, the quickness of it—it is difficult to step back and see strategies or dynamics that aren't healthy and that could cause problems later on. By slowing down, learning to be a better listener, and making decisions from a clearer, more lucid, and grounded place, I think a mindfulness practice helps me be a wiser actor. It can provide practical tools to keep myself grounded in the hotness of a difficult situation and, hopefully, to sway energies in a way that is more generative. To not lose myself to my anger and not be blinded by it. There are a lot of reasons to be outraged, but I have also seen how I've been carried away by my rage, that it's sometimes limited my view. I have had to contend with moments when I haven't made the best, wisest decisions in certain difficult moments. It's also helped me work on cleansing my own heart and helped me approach my work with more kindness and generosity.

I think political action requires a vision but also solid, consistent steps and actions. It requires that we stay rooted amid the tumult happening around us. To have a clear vision in difficult times and to be in the moment but also still have our eyes on the larger vision. That's not easy to do. So, yes, for me, Buddhist practices have helped me build a toolbox to be that actor. I'm not going to be arrogant: I have a long way to go. But I feel more equipped.

I can distinguish between what I need to deal with on my own versus what is social. Certain traumas I need to tend to on my own, not in an activist space or in an organizing campaign or event. Sometimes we don't know that. I've definitely seen people, organizers and activists, whose own trauma can take up a lot of space and gets played out in the name of politics when there may be something more personal unfolding.

This is a little difficult. I want to be concrete and I don't want to speak in abstractions. But I don't really want to get into the specifics of problematic instances in organizing efforts I've been a part of.

DW: I have a more positive question to ask. Maybe it brings us to a natural closure. You've used the word "sangha," a Sanskrit term meaning the community of Buddhist practitioners, people who seek together or in common purpose, formally or informally. So many of your projects are either direct collaborations or forms of public engagement. Can you draw connections between the way you approach art making in terms of who you're trying to bring together as compared to the ideals of sangha—as a refuge, as a place of mutual support, as a vehicle for shared spiritual travel? Is there a comparison to be made between the way we think about collective experience when it comes to a creative project, for example, your works that activate participation, and the work of building sangha, one of the Three Jewels offered in Buddhist practice? Or are these social formations different, related, or both?

    I wonder how you view these two modes of being together with people, of finding people with whom to share either a struggle or a path.

SL: Thank you. I don't know if I see a whole lot of difference between holding sangha in my studio/living room/little meditation space, and my more outward work as an artist organizing a socially engaged event, or whatever form my own artistic practice may take. Actually, what drew me into cultural practice in the early 1990s was the tangibility of creating other spaces that did not exist in a city like Los Angeles, in the United States, in a capitalist economy. Urban space is designed for us to be workers, consumers, to be landowners or renters. Culture and our social relationships are so defined by our roles in these structures. I'm interested in the questions, How and where do we find freedom? How and where do we create paths toward liberation? How do we transform those structures? How do we claim them? How do we occupy them differently?

    Both sangha and my artistic practice are about creating spaces to allow us to discover parts of ourselves, parts that don't fit the physical or social roles demanded by the structures of urban space. Feeding and growing these other selves allows us to recognize and see each other in other ways, to be with each other in other ways, and to love each other in other ways. I am interested in tools, whether it be through the breath or through a

EXHALING PEACE

spray can, or a turntable and a needle in an empty space where we can dance and inhabit our bodies differently, to imagine, to dream, to tap into the deeper recesses of ourselves, to remember, rediscover, reclaim our ancestral legacies and practices, especially as those of various Indigenous diasporas. Those reserves of knowledge, cultivating and sharing those knowledge practices, keeping them alive, connecting with the land, with the earth—I think they are all one and the same. The tools of sitting, breathing, and listening are parallel with the tools of a paintbrush, of printmaking, or a camera, or a guitar, or our bodies in dance, or whatever creative tools we may use in art and cultural spaces.

This interview took place on January 31, 2021.

ASYNCHRONOUS LINGERING AND THE CAPILLARIES OF CARE

Pato Hebert

What a civilian would call their dining room is what I call my artist studio in Los Angeles. In order to make it semifunctional as my creative work space, for years I've gone without a specific space to eat in. Yet, now, eighteen months into the COVID-19 pandemic, it has fully devolved into a hovel of unnavigable clutter. So much there feels heavy, neglected, languishing—the nascent watercolor project about football concussions stopped cold by the start of COVID, stacks of books I'd hoped to read but could never quite crack, debts I've yet to deal with.

Taped to a bookshelf in the corner of the space are printouts of screen grabs. They burst with nurturing guidance from a former student-turned-friend. From the locked-down epicenter of Brooklyn, she sent me breathing exercises, encouragement, and care. Daniel Tucker, one of the coeditors of this volume, saw a post I'd made about it on social media and gently suggested I consider including the instructions as part of my submission to this collection. So I decided to digitally revisit the original message from my supportive friend. I was struck by how consistently she has reached out during my illness and how extensive our exchanges were. I didn't remember any of these vital and sustaining communiqués until I scrolled through my DMs.

I got sick with COVID-19 during the pandemic's early push in the United States. By the spring of 2020, I was already part of the first wave of long haulers—folks who remained ill weeks after initial infection and did not quickly, easily, or completely recover.

I am writing this in July 2021. Yesterday, I had a follow-up with my neurologist to track my slow but steady progress. I'm trying to figure out when to see the gastroenterologist again to contend with my persistent digestive flare-ups. The refill of my inhaler prescription is delayed due to insurance issues. Some of my tinctures and powdered supplements also need to be reordered. And I'm a few weeks behind on acupuncture.

But it is the care of friends and loved ones that is the regenerative tissue of my uneven recovery. Even just this one friend's persistent efforts are voluminous, humbling, and invaluable. When I first got sick last spring, she sent me a care package with a homemade beaded coaster and her original stickers, plus her mother's recipe for healing soup. It arrived via a circular Forever stamp featuring the full moon and scalloped edges. I live for snail mail.

It took me weeks to muster the energy to send a brief digital thank you. On May 24, 2020, I wrote:

> I'm up and down. Better last few days after some relapse setbacks last week. Daily walks in park helping, and unexpectedly generating new series of images of fallen PPE. Lots of writing and editing deadlines have now mostly cleared. Need to tend to my own infrastructure and body before school starts up again. Poco a poco.

On June 25, 2020, she DMed me the breathing exercises that I later printed out and taped up in my dysfunctional studio. She wrote:

> I used to do an exercise with a PT for quelling panic responses while running and also while not running. I felt like it taught me how to feel like I had control over my oxygen when it felt like my heart or lungs weren't working.
>
> These exercises train the tissues of the lungs and abdomen to stretch and contract as well as the body to utilize the oxygen it has available to it in the bloodstream.
>
> We began conservatively with the tempo breathing. A day/week/month (or however long it takes to feel comfortable to progress). Then moved to the maximal breathing. Then breath holding. The latter two options are more bodily stressful.
>
> — Tempo breathing to develop control and promote parasympathetic response:
>
>   • In for 4 seconds, out for 4 (4 sets)
>   • In for 4, out for 6 (4 sets)
>   • In for 4, out for 8 (4 sets)
>
> — Maximal expansive/contractive breathing
>
>   • Inhale fully and hold for 1-2 sec, then inhale a little more. Repeat 1-3x before exhaling.
>   • Exhale fully and continue exhaling even when the lungs feel empty. Hold for 1-2 sec. Repeat 1-3x before inhaling.

> > > > > > > > > >

Breath holding:

— With inhaled lungs

  • Take a big inhale and hold.
  • Start with a goal of 60 sec. Add intervals of 15 or 30 sec as you feel capable. Try to reassure the stressful thoughts that arises that all is well and the next breath is there whenever you need it, so you can safely challenge yourself if you want to.

— With exhaled lungs

  • Take a big inhale in to fully expand the lungs, and then fully and normally exhale all of the air out. Do not inhale again. Hold as long as possible. Aim for 30 sec to begin with. Add intervals of 15 to progress.

The next day I DMed her back:

Thank you. Breath. Movement. Exhaling anxiety. Next moments. So important.

In September I underwent still further exams to determine if I've had a stroke and if there was any structural damage to my brain. More of her care streamed into my DMs, with loving offers to study the exam images together. I replied:

You're so thoughtful! Definitely would love to geek out about this at some point.

For now save your precious energy on hustling labs. I've already had EKG, CT scan, ultrasound, and yesterday an MRI and comprehensive pulmonary exam. So now I just need to get results and discuss w specialists. It will all be okay.

I am, however, in love with ultrasound equipment.
I really want one!

How are you holding up?

Even as my bills kept piling up and my long COVID
persisted, I kept having the strange fantasy of getting
an artist residency that would somehow come with
access to ultrasound gear. I wanted to make images of
the inside of this body that had long since had to make
room for the virus and its aftereffects.

Later, in December, my friend messaged that
she'd had a nightmare about my medical bills as she
juggled her own years of debt stemming from a surgery.
She said her surgeon's financial manager actually kept
pushing off the conversation about costs because they
were worried about it affecting her recovery, which, she
noted, "is so ironic and emblematic!"

Now, halfway into year two of the pandemic, I still
can't do those held-breath exercises. But I no longer
take my inhaler every day, and I only need the emergency
inhaler one or two times per month. If sports first schooled
me to mind my breathing in my youth, and Buddhism
later taught me how to further listen to and hone it in my
30s, my friend's consistent care was and is part of a huge
ecosystem of sustenance that helps me to survive COVID.

***

During these sixteen months of sickness, my corporeal
compass has skewed. Time frequently slips its register.
This is a protracted and frustrating process that I call
the COVIDoldrums. Yet creativity and care endure. The
early images that I wrote to her about in the spring
of 2020 have now become the Lingering series, part of
which is presented here.

When I first got sick, I had to stop working on
numerous sculptural, painting, and text-based works.
Like so many other artists, I saw COVID cancel my
exhibitions, trips, and presentations. But it also radically

impacted my own sense of pace and possibility. I had to recalibrate my creative research to a body whose rhythms and capacities were greatly altered by the virus, a body that cannot be understood as mine. COVID exerts its own temporal asymmetries and pressures, its sneak attacks and subterfuges. It is not linear or easily predictable. Its hallmark is uncertainty.

The coronavirus continues to wreak havoc via variants and deviants. Despite the immense privilege and increasing protection of broad vaccine access, the US has now surpassed six hundred thousand COVID deaths. The finality of these deaths is one COVID time register. The timeline of the grieving to come is another. Still another is the expanding and difficult-to-measure horizon of the long hauler. One in three people infected become long haulers. This means that in the US alone we can estimate there are now ten million of us. The scale is staggering, the timeframe for recovery unclear and bewildering.

Yet in the face of the coronavirus onslaught, we also experience and embrace the half-life of hope, the life force that so often seems to fade throughout the pandemic but that can—like my friend's care—also somehow persist. Los Angeles was one of the hardest-hit places on the planet at the start of 2021. Six months later, California now has one of the lowest infection rates in the world, but LA County has encouraged mask wearing as an additional protection against (re)infection. Vaccines have intensified the fact that different jurisdictions live in different COVID temporalities. The virus is not the same in any two bodies, nor in any two locales. How do we therefore understand the textures and temporality of recovery?

This question has me thinking about how we practice multiple forms of care, for the self and with others. Our resilience can range from mutual-aid efforts to exercise. For decades LA's Elysian Park has been utilized by Latinx families, young people, elders, and queer people, as well as multiple immigrant communities. Jogging, dog walking, and socially distanced picnics are just some of the activities that continued to proliferate during the worst parts of the pandemic, the park offering precious public space and respite.

When the mayor first closed the pools and gyms in March 2020, I started walking in Elysian Park. This was also where I accessed a free COVID-19 public testing site on March 24. And the park is where I returned once I finally had enough energy to take my first slow, gentle, fifteen-minute walk during my initial recuperation in April 2020. Since then, regular two-mile walks in the park have become integral to my gradual recovery process. Walking can be counterproductive for many long haulers. But for me, when done with measure, it often helps. Initially, I tried to add five additional minutes to my walk each day, incremental adjustments that anxiously probed the body's limits. This, too, was COVID time, and these walks were and are a lifesaver. They have slowly helped me to rebuild my lung capacity and strengthen my spirit.

Elysian Park is a hilly beacon of six hundred acres located right in the heart of the city. Free and accessible during daylight hours, its trails, breezes, and embrace have been even more vital to the city's wellness practices during the pandemic. It is a special place that has been integral to my own process of healing and creativity. It has nuanced my sense of time—from the geological and topographical time embodied by the bedrock to seasonal shifts in temperatures, flowers, and migrating birds, to the ephemera of fallen PPE littering the landscape. These different scales of time unfold as I stumble to comprehend the unevenness of this body, whose clock so seldom seems to have any regularity of schedule.

The raw, expansive park also offers the gift of images. Reminders of the pandemic are everywhere. The park is marked by people's protection and affection, care and pleasure. I have been making pictures with my mobile phone during my walks. The images presence the virus's impact on our lives, our impact on the park, and the persistence of the park's land as a vibrant force.

It is difficult to express the depth of my gratitude for the care that this land has offered me—the challenge of its inclines, the company of its coyotes, the lessons of its life cycles, the embrace of its folds.

Across contemporary media, I have found that too little has been written or created from the perspective of artists and people infected with the novel coronavirus, even as our ranks continue to grow by the thousands every day worldwide. Most of us are too tired and are just trying to survive. These Lingering images work against this silence to evoke the masses of people who are navigating the strangeness and immense uncertainty of COVID-19. This work is also an ongoing thank you to all those beings—both human and more than human—who nudge and nurture us toward health. This is neither an impatient race to embrace a post-pandemic state nor a default into ableist notions of wellness. Rather, as I did with my friend's guidance, I am marveling at the capillaries of connection and care as we navigate the pandemic's ensuing chapters together.

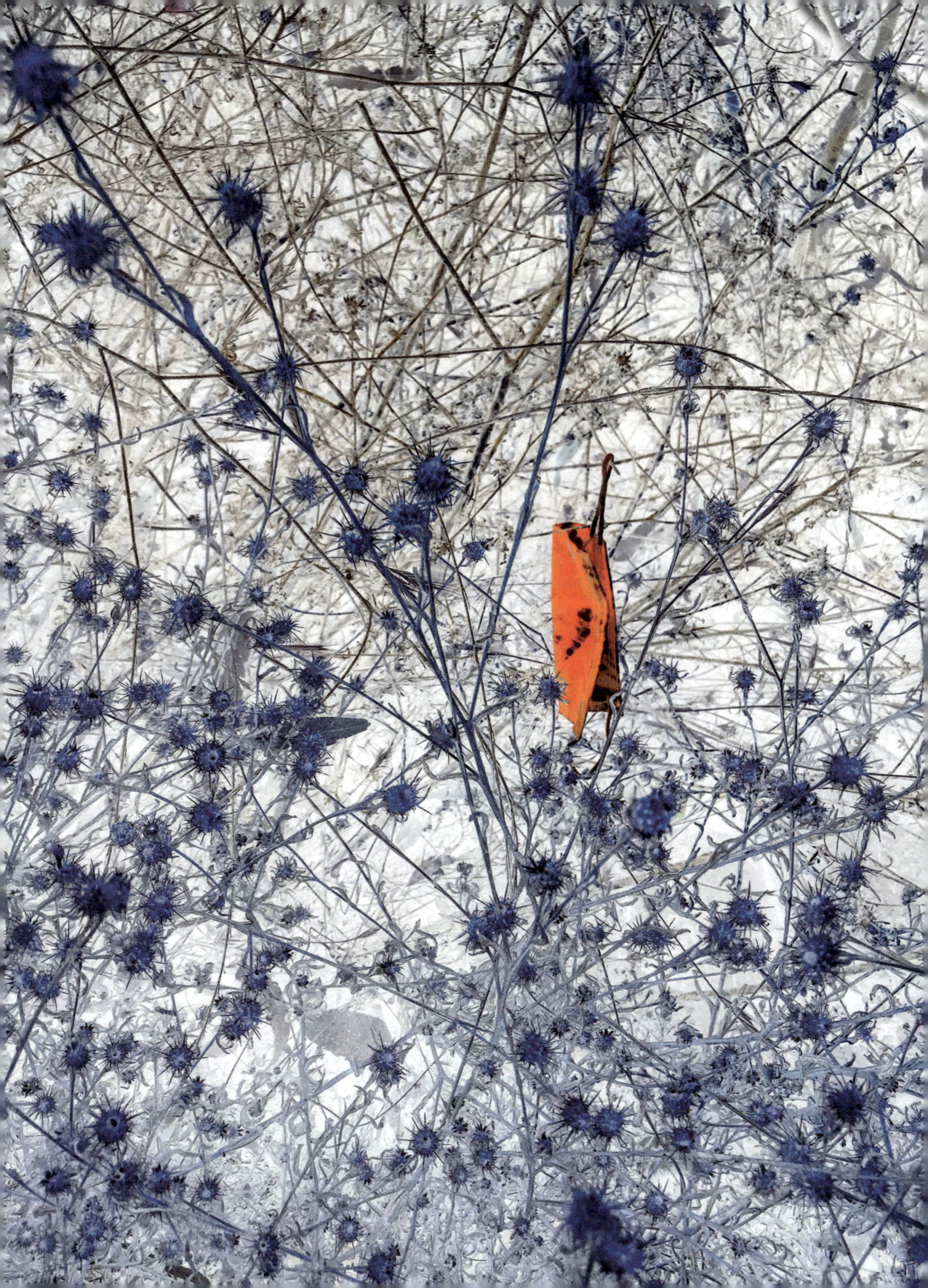

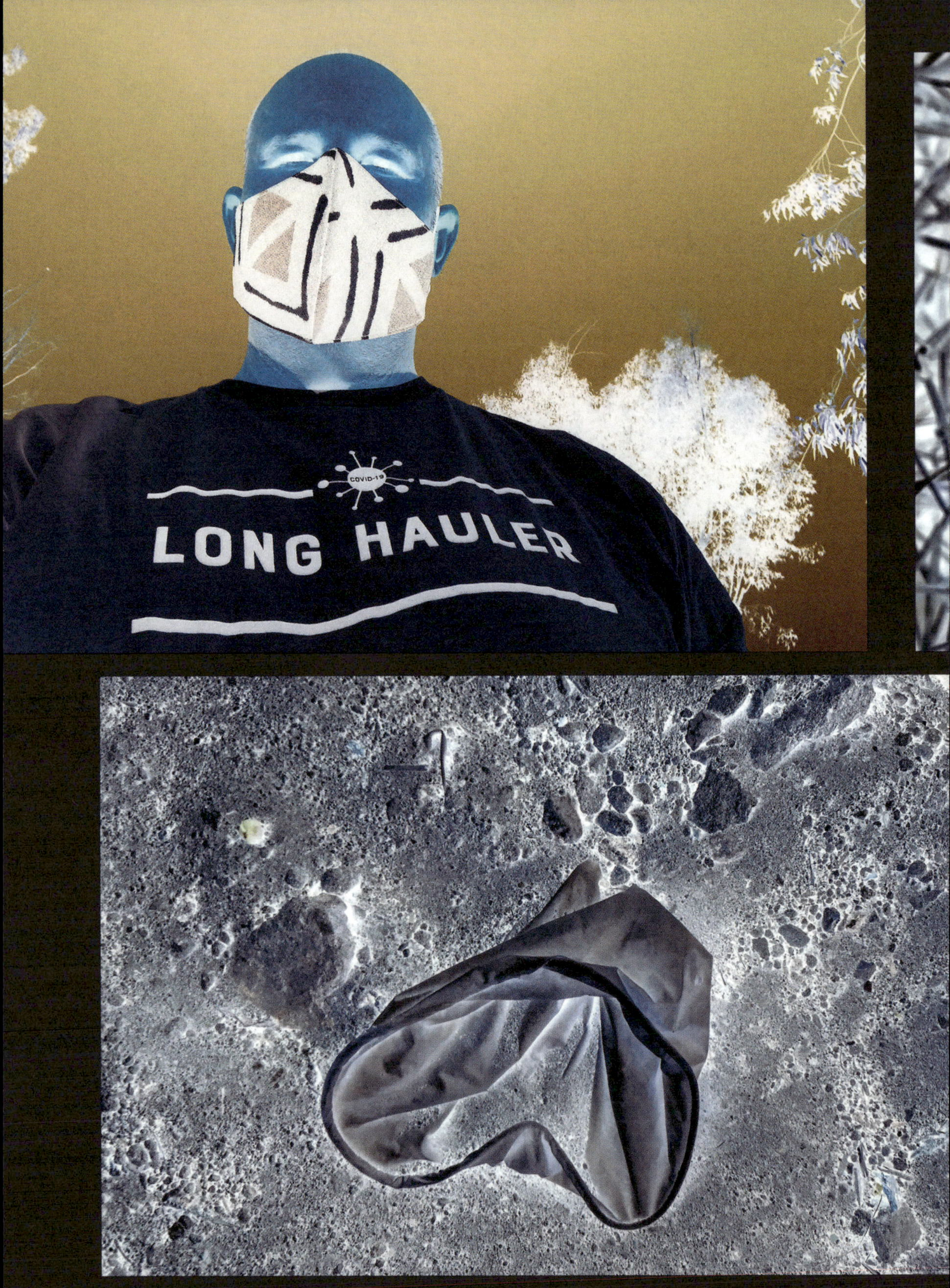
COVID-19
LONG HAULER

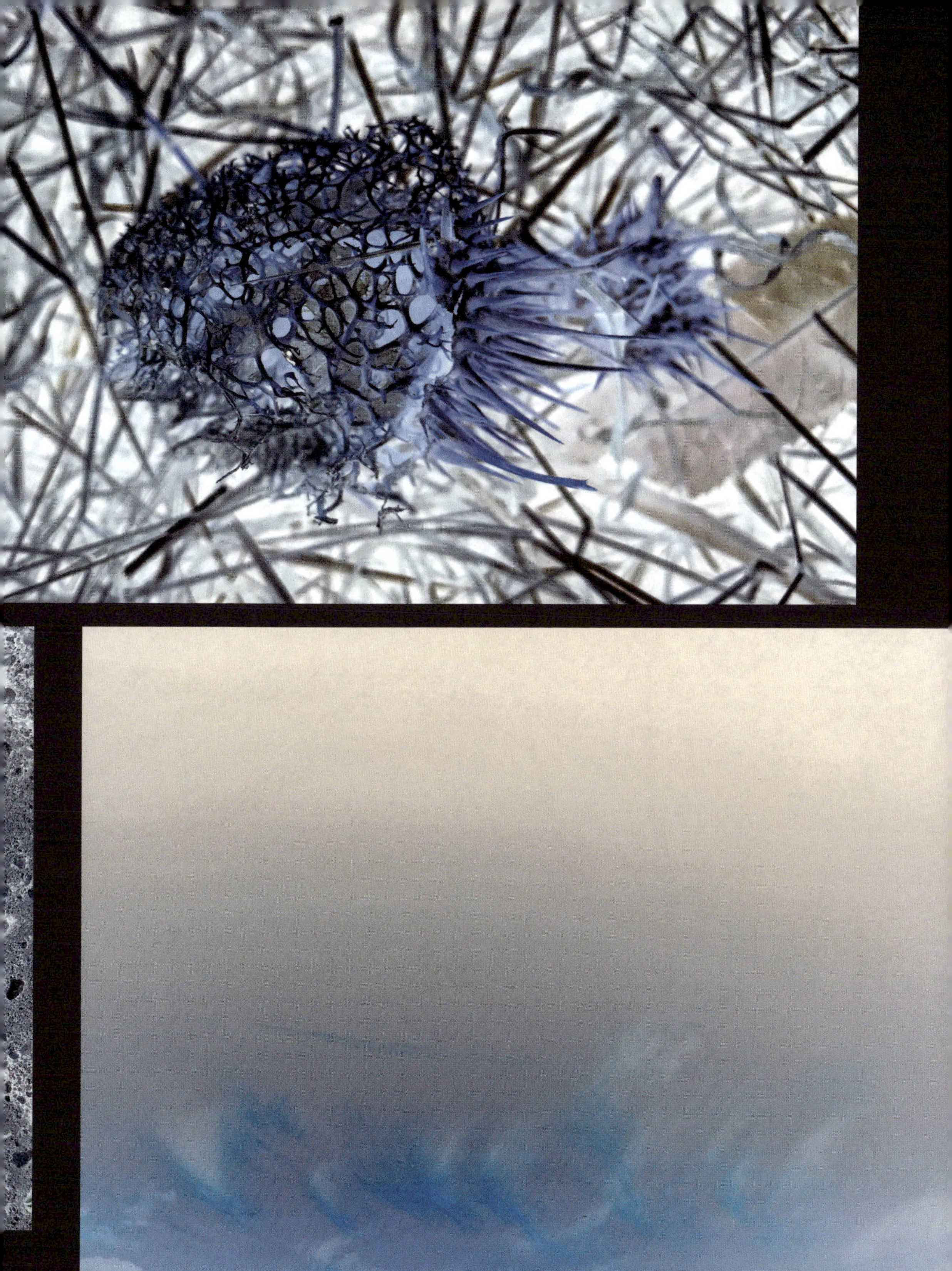

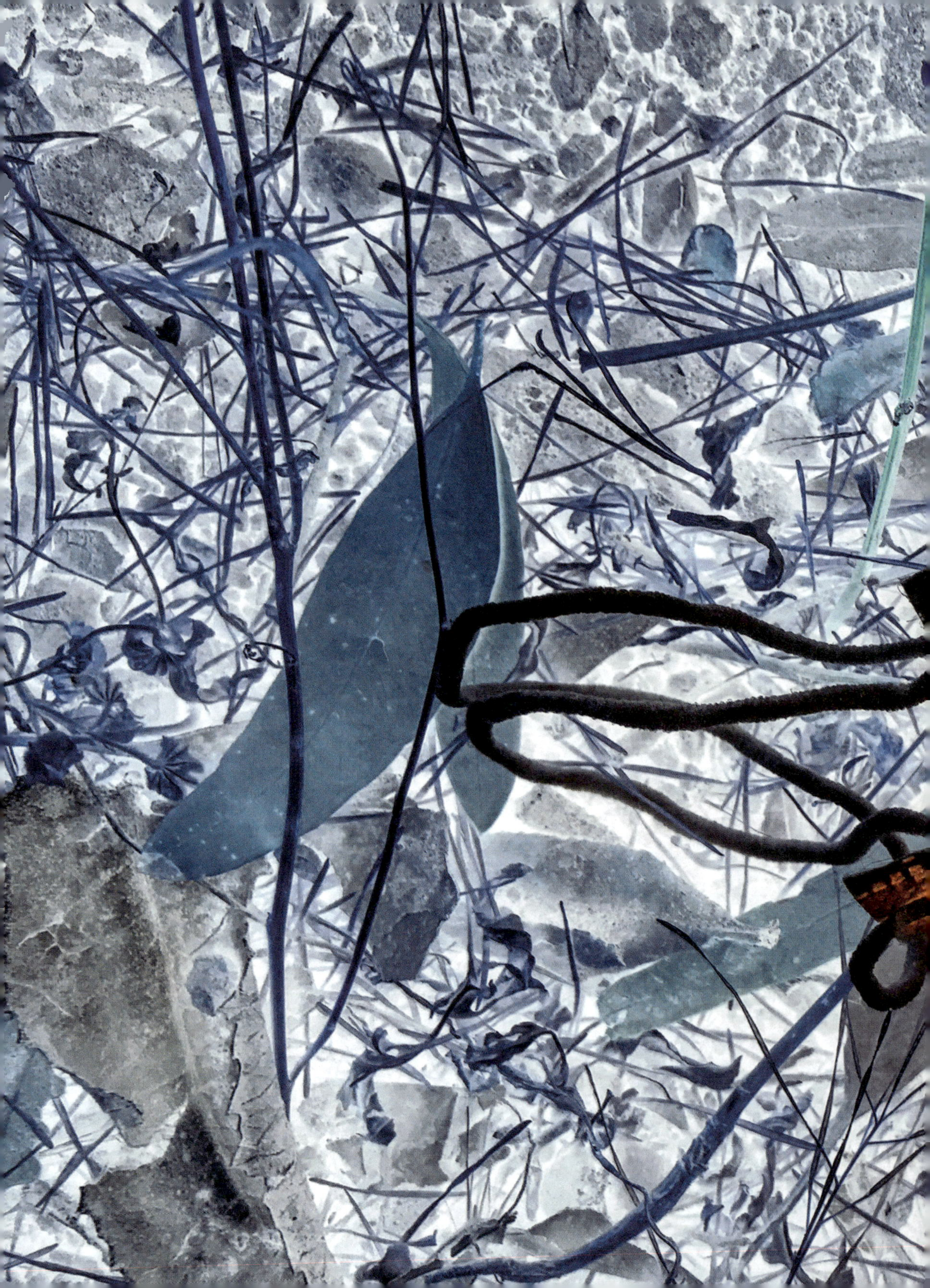

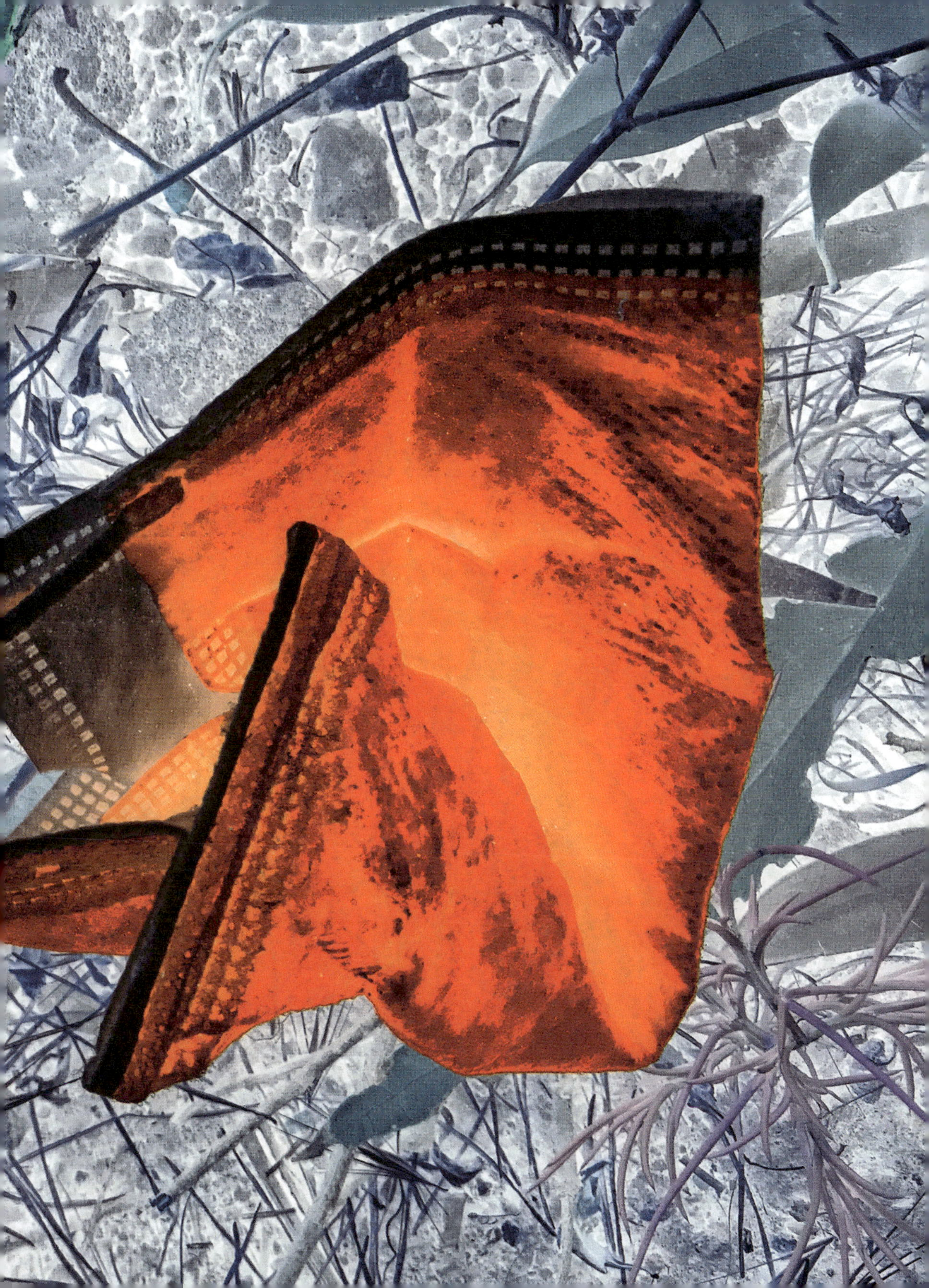

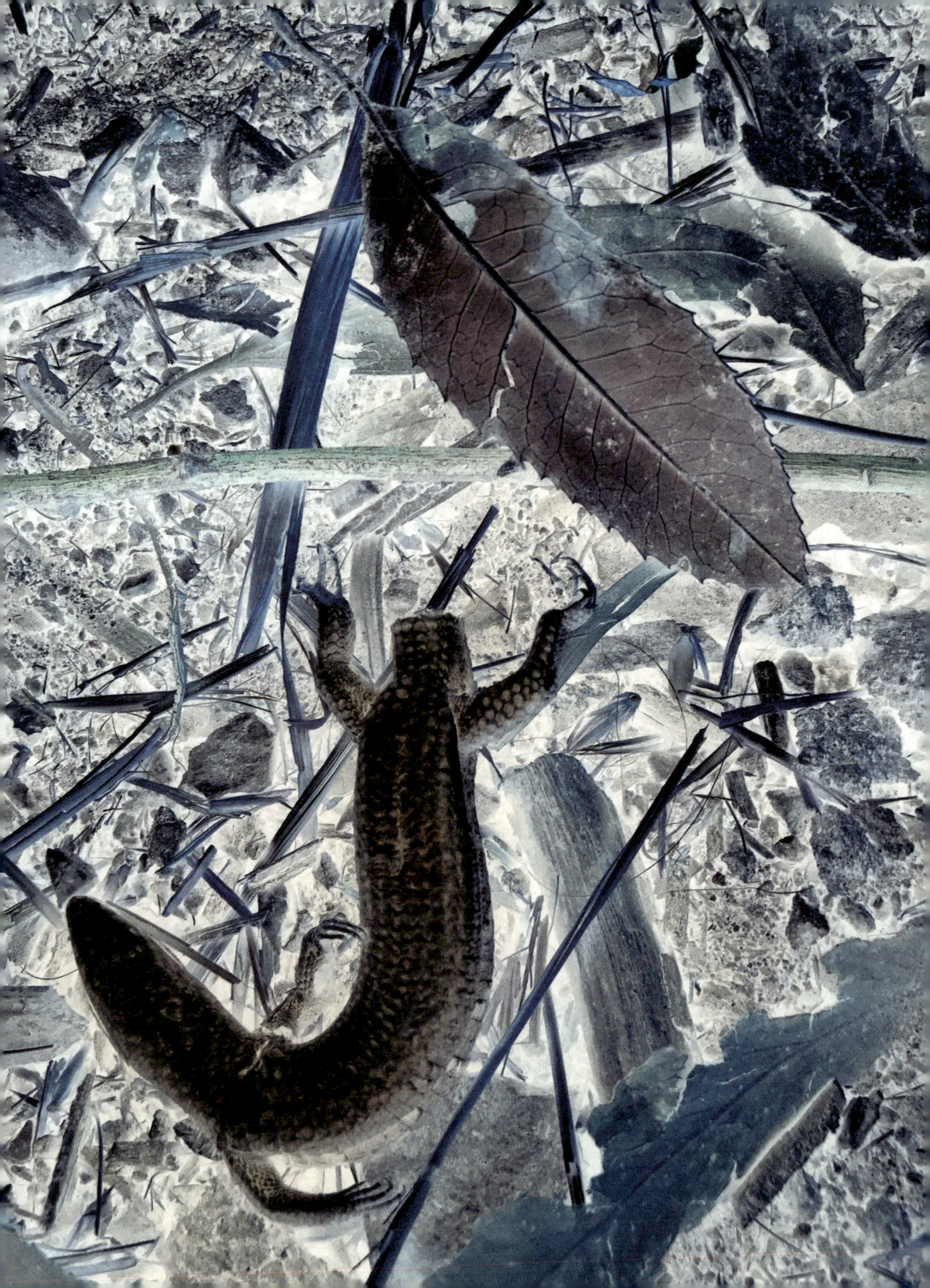

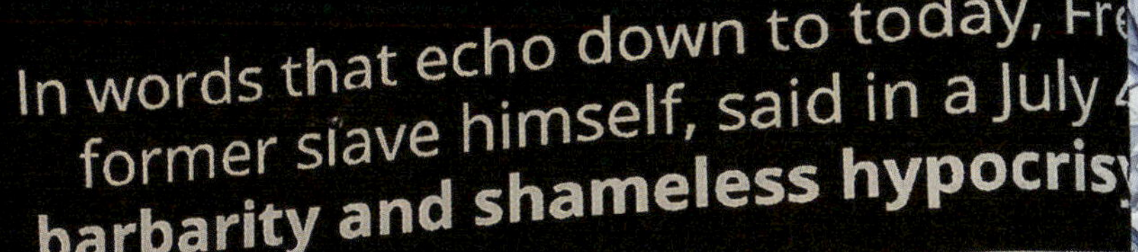

In words that echo down to today, Fre[derick Douglass,]
former slave himself, said in a July 4[th speech of the]
barbarity and shameless hypocris[y...]

This July 4th: De[...]
to Dishonor the[...]

WE
DEMAND:

AN END TO INS[...]
AND MURDER [...]

AN END TO AN[...]
USED, ABUSED, [...]

WE NEED: REVOLUT[ION]

The U.S.A. was founded on enslavement of Black [...]
expanded through war stealing large parts of Me[xico's]
land.

The U.S.A.'s wealth and power has since been bu[ilt...]
followed by a New Jim Crow of mass incarceratio[n...]
as well as world-wide plunder, conquest, CIA co[...]

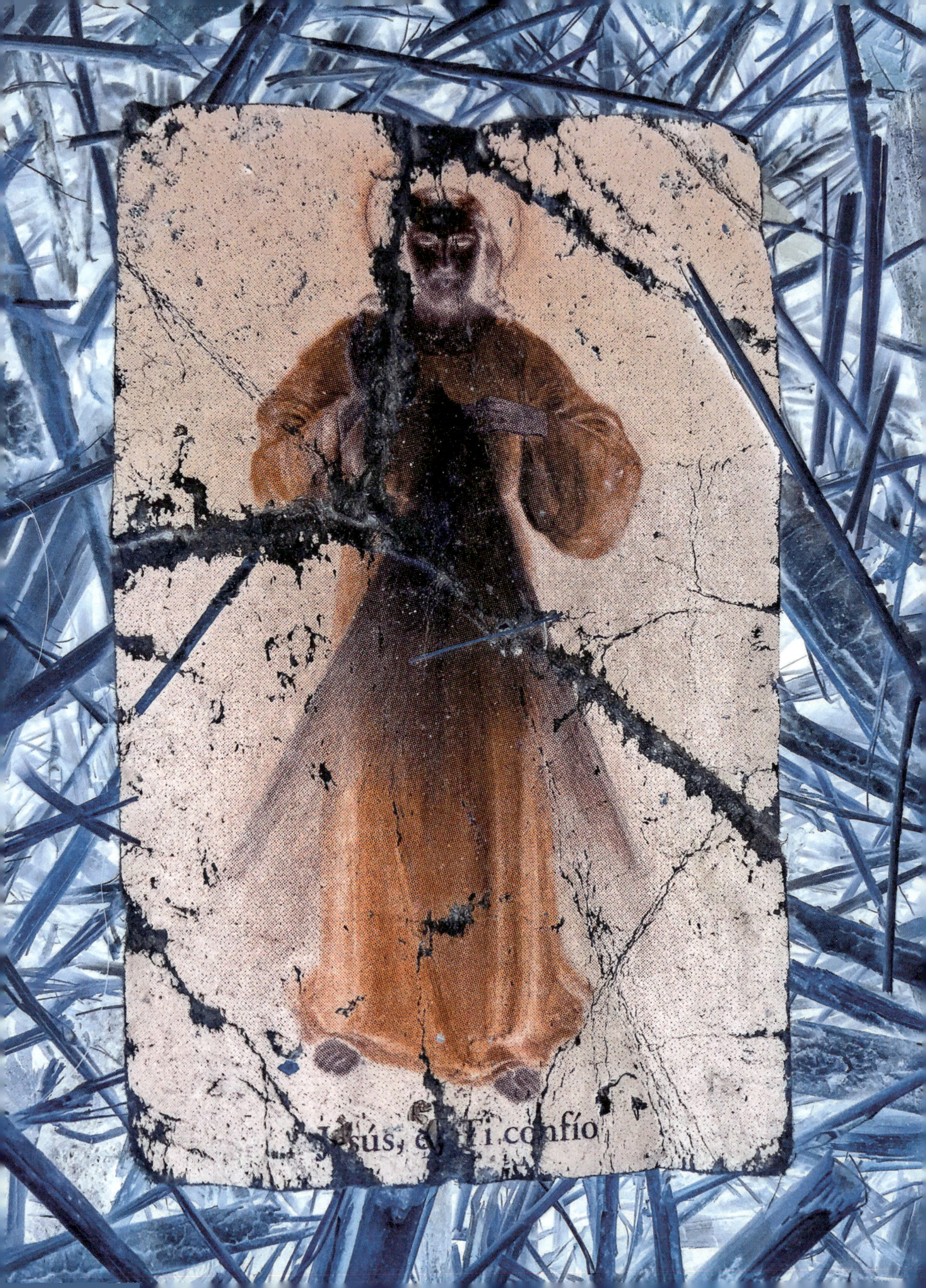

Jesús, en Ti confío

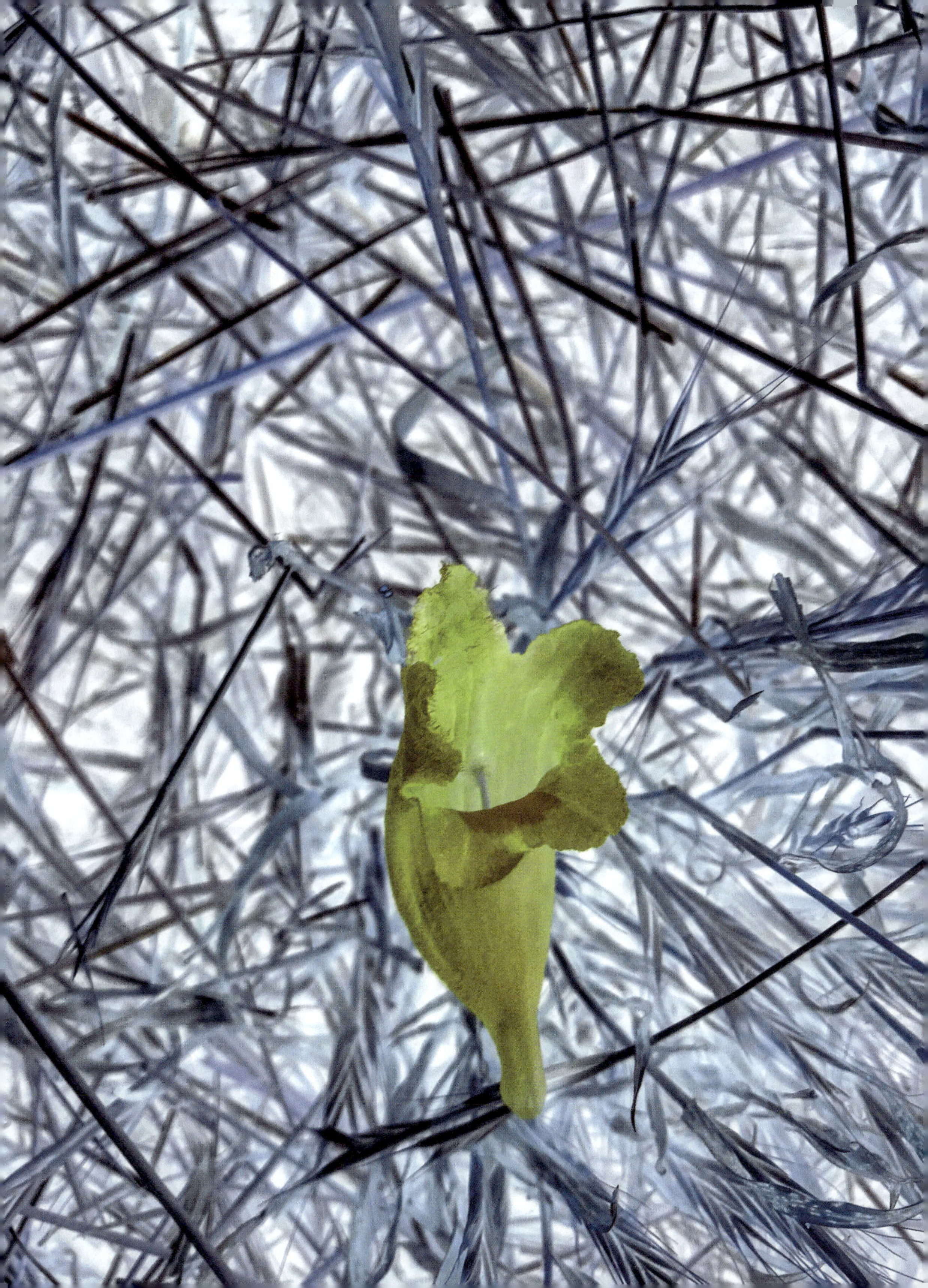

CARE IN CRISIS

Daniel Tucker

One after another after another. Artist Alicia Grullón spent the early days of the pandemic in March 2020 trying to count ambulance sirens. She lives near a hospital in the Bronx, a borough of New York City, and the cases in her area eventually rose to over ten thousand by mid-April, the highest rate of hospitalization and death resulting from COVID-19 in the city. Counting became impossible.[1]

Grullón later reflected that "it simply got to be too many at a time, and I did not want to normalize any of it because the overall handling of the crisis had been abysmal. Another week in, I stopped looking at the time. COVID broke what was familiar to me . . . Aside from immediate family living with me, the only other human beings I would see were essential workers."[2]

The term "essential workers" emerged as a part of the pandemic lexicon, but it actually originated during World War I. The concept was used to recognize the workers who performed duties required for basic domestic survival and the "all-out production" necessitated by the war effort. In the context of COVID-19, the category was expanded, offering an opportunity to value work that was historically lower paid and increasingly hazardous, from grocery store workers to health care workers.[3]

While it could be argued that "care" also became a key word in the pandemic lexicon, in my experience as an educator it had emerged in recent years as a

1
See R. K. Wadhera et al., "Variation in COVID-19 Hospitalizations and Deaths across New York City Boroughs," *JAMA* 321, no. 21 (April 2020): 2192–95, doi:10.1001/jama.2020.7197.

2
Alicia Grullón, "Hot City: At Home with Essential Workers," *Verso* (blog), August 27, 2020, https://www.versobooks.com/blogs/4841-hot-city-at-home-with-essential-workers.

3
Jennifer Klein, "Essential Workers—Definition, History, and Importance," WSHU, September 25, 2020, https://www.wshu.org/post/essential-work-ers-definition-history-and-im-portance#stream/0.

4

Student projects on this theme included "Levels of Care" (@levels.of.care), Instagram, 2021, https:// www.instagram.com/levels. of.care/; and "Care Crisis: A Time Capsule about Art & Curating during a Pandemic from Students at Moore College of Art & Design," Care Crisis WordPress, 2021, https://carecrisis. wordpress.com/.

5

"Nearly One-Third of U.S. Coronavirus Deaths Are Linked to Nursing Homes," *New York Times*, June 2, 2021, https://www.nytimes. com/interactive/2020/us/ coronavirus-nursing-homes. html.

6

"Ai-Jen Poo: The Work that Makes All Other Work Possible," Ted.com, December 7, 2018, https:// www.ted.com/talks/ai_jen_ poo_the_work_that_makes_ all_other_work_possible.

framework that appealed to students as a way to grapple with and update the feminist project of exploring the interconnectedness of the personal and the political.[4] "Care" was also already on the tongues of a growing number of social theorists, artists, and community organizers, alike, in the language connecting the struggles involving health, domestic life, the organization of time, and the visibility of the marginalized workers who keep society functioning, which Grullón's statement so elegantly captures.

While COVID-19 touched everyone, what it felt like individually had everything to do with where one was located at the intersection of class, race, and geography. The pandemic also laid bare the contradictions of age, disability, and even nutrition: Nursing homes were flooded with the virus, representing the largest concentration of death tolls at 40 percent of the nation's total (for both residents and workers).[5] Disabled people, who had fought for generations to get publicly funded support for their independence, were now navigating new vulnerabilities and abandonment. Food workers, from farmers to delivery workers and grocery store cashiers, became "essential" overnight as food insecurity rose. People stranded at home felt their bodies in new ways after the numbing business of staying busy had come to a halt; some discovered self-care, others suffered. Kids were sent home from schools, leaving their parents to perform childcare and teaching roles, or not, depending on their status as workers-from-home, essential, or unemployed. This event suddenly woke everyone to what the artists and activists in this chapter have been saying for years.

The projects profiled below give a sense of how artists in urban contexts have used performance to take on the intersecting issues found within urban health care, before and now during the pandemic. Moving across essential work, elder care, food access, and self-care, their practices support increased visibility for "the work that makes all other work possible," as care work advocate Ai-Jen Poo frequently reminds us.[6]

Elder Boom!

As far as catalytic events go, getting older is about as slow as an event can get when compared with a sweeping global pandemic. But the "elder boom" is gradually advancing, and, by 2030, there will have been a 75 percent increase in the number of Americans aged sixty-five and older. This will move the people in need of nursing assistance or home health care to about 2.3 million in 2030, up from 1.3 million in 2010.

This development, combined with changes in work and health care, has created the conditions in which care work has become one of the fastest growing sectors in the US economy. One recent report projected that between 2016 and 2026, a "41 percent growth in employment for home health aides and personal care aides, compared with an average of 7 percent growth for all occupations."[7] If you add people providing care for children and cleaning homes as part of the larger "care economy," then the numbers of people who are implicated as workers and consumers entangled in care is massive.

Recent years have brought about a resurgence in "human reproduction theory," which has sought to theorize the ways in which care work is required to reproduce the very existence of the waged worker, of future workers (children), and of the former worker (elders). One prominent thinker, author Silvia Federici, wrote of the international Wages for Housework campaign in 1975 that "We must admit that capital has been very successful in hiding our work." She continued, "To say that we want wages for housework is to expose the fact that housework is already money for capital, that capital has made and makes money out of our cooking, smiling, fucking."[8] As women have increasingly worked outside of the home since Federici's first writing, this condition has surely changed, partially through the invisible labor of domestic work that has filled in that gap of unpaid labor with low-paid labor.

These changes in the household division of labor have a significant impact on the culture of families and

[7] Cynthia Hess and Ariane Hegewisch, "The Future of Care Work: Improving the Quality of America's Fastest-Growing Jobs," The Institute for Women's Policy Research (IWPR), 2019, https://iwpr.org/wp-content/uploads/2020/07/C486_Future-of-Care-Work_final.pdf.

[8] Silvia Federici, *Wages against Housework* (Bristol: Power of Women Collective and Falling Wall Press, 1975), PDF available from Caring Labor: An Archive, https://caringlabor.files.wordpress.com/2010/11/federici-wages-against-housework.pdf.

produce precarious interdependencies between people who are unrelated and live in dramatically different social conditions. Increasingly, a national movement has mobilized that is focused on "caregivers," mostly women of color, working across the care continuum, from nannies providing child care to the home aides and housekeepers who cook, clean, and perform health tasks for people needing assistance. While mostly about workers—the term encompasses some individual employers of care workers as well—it is essentially people who "care about care" as a compelling, broad, and intersectional framework that has echoes of the last decades of day-labor and farmworker organizing, which sought to bring workers out of the shadows. Moreover, this work of making labor visible can also be applied to those on the receiving end of care, as in the following art projects and practices.

Well before the pandemic, there had been a dramatic increase in arts programming about, by, and for aging populations. One early adopter was theater artist Anne Basting. Basting founded Timeslips in 1998 and since then has used the organization as a platform for continued work in senior homes and with people living with dementia, particularly in the city of Milwaukee. In 2014, after several successful projects inside nursing homes and elsewhere, Basting took a ride around Milwaukee's south side, in the Bayview neighborhood where her grandmother grew up, with a local Meals on Wheels program. In Bayview, as in many cities, older adults live alone and the social isolation can be deadly (the 739 mostly elderly deaths of the Chicago heat wave of 1995 was a tragic wake-up call to this pattern). As Basting wrote: "We knew we could bring meaning and connection to a care community, where staffing and daily routines provided infrastructure for creativity. But bringing meaning and connection to people in their homes would be a bigger lift. We'd need to figure out how to deliver the spark and how to gather it back."[9]

After several ride-alongs, during which Basting was able to see the meal-delivery system at work, the

9
Anne Basting, "From Islands to Archipelagos," in *Creative Care* (New York: HarperOne, 2020), 163.

Islands of Milwaukee project emerged, which was as simple and elegant as the routine delivery itself. Time is of the essence with these service initiatives, so Basting's project needed to fit right into the delivery flow without disruption and without imposing on the senior client or the delivery person. The driver would ask the meal recipient if they wanted to receive the question of the day and, if they did, they would be given a card with a question written on it. They could either reply by phone through a voicemail service, or they could write out a reply and return it when the next delivery arrived. For months the project went on like that. Questions ranged from "What's the most beautiful sound in your home?" to "What could you teach another person?" to "Is there an intersection you would like to cross but [it] feels dangerous?"

Some 2,500 replies came in response to forty-five questions, by voicemail and card. The results were edited into a radio series that aired over several weeks with hopes that the participants would hear their replies being read. This was eventually developed into a performance event by Sojourn Theater at Milwaukee's City Hall wherein replies were read and more collected.

Basting later wrote that the seniors' social isolation had shed light on another issue, which led to another project: "Many older adults receiving meals live across the street from food sources. But the street, to a disabled elder, was completely impassable." And so, in 2015, *The Crossing*, a performance project, also realized with the collaboration of Sojourn Theater, took on dangerous intersections with a parade of visibility in the form of a dispersed "sailboat" of bodies, waving flags and ringing bells. The parade members carried signs that read, simply, "Thank you for seeing and stopping for pedestrians."[10] While it may be impractical to imagine a parade of strangers accompanying every senior who crosses a dangerous intersection, there is potential in making visible and collective what are often private and debilitating fears.

Basting recently reflected that, after years of trying to reframe long-term care facilities as cultural

10
Anne Basting, "The Crossings," Anne Basting (website), 2015, https://www.anne-basting.com/projects.

centers with porous boundaries, when the pandemic lockdown happened, all the boundaries became rigid. She described the pain that people experienced when they had to connect with loved ones through windows. Her organization led webinars on ways to build connections amid the lockdowns. Basting suggested that "as much work as we have to do with white privilege and racial inequities, we have to do the same work with aging and ableism as well."[11] COVID-19's impact on interpersonal care, rendering touch and breath as potential dangers, has offered an opportunity to speak more tangibly about interdependence.

In a Zoom program early in the pandemic, Ai Jen Poo engaged in a dialogue with disability rights activists. The discussion explored how disability was a part of all of our movements for justice and that focusing on it would help us to discuss specifically long-term care needs, as well as interdependence more broadly. Poo spoke about the way disability activists had influenced her thinking about supporting interdependence and dignity, emphasizing that one of the key lessons from the movement was to "demand what you deserve. . . . From the beginning this movement was about asserting your full value and humanity. Sometimes we are trained to ask for what we think we can get and it is usually not sufficient." She went on to explain that this moment offers us an opportunity to be more intentional about showing what we value, asserting, "I believe that [care]... is a public good and we should invest in it that way."[12]

Community Care

Walking into the Free People's Medical Clinic, a project by artist Simone Leigh, visitors were greeted by costumed nurses who guided them into various spaces of a historic mansion dedicated to themes of community care. The waiting room was decorated with fliers for yoga and healthy free meals, and a wide range of

11
Anne Basting, "Conversations@Moore: Art & Aging," Conversations@Moore Archive, 2021, https://conversationsarchive.wordpress.com/2021/02/09/anne-basting/.

12
Ai-Jen Poo, Judy Heumann, and Nikki Brown-Booker, "Crip Camp: The Fight for Disability & Domestic Worker Rights," (presentation, Hand-in-Hand: The Network of Domestic Employers' public program, Thursday, July 2, 2020), https://domesticworkers.zoom.us/rec/play/6ZYol-er9_z83HNWStgSDVqR-6W9S6JqKshilW8_oJx-R7gWiEHYwDyY7USZuRb-RlcYXxflibFb4yzWRl3.

experiences to which visitors could return in the expansive home known as Stuyvesant Mansion.

Located in the Crown Heights neighborhood of Brooklyn, Stuyvesant Mansion was once home to Dr. Josephine English, the first African American woman to establish an OB/GYN practice in the state of New York; she delivered around six thousand babies, including the children of Malcolm X and Betty Shabazz.[13] Many years earlier, Dr. Susan Smith McKinney Steward, the first Black woman to earn a medical degree and work as a physician in New York state, lived and worked in the same neighborhood. When Steward was born, this part of Crown Heights was known as Weeksville, a neighborhood founded by free African Americans in the 1830s.

Because of this history, the Weeksville Heritage Center worked with the public art organization Creative Time in 2014 to present the multisite exhibition *FunkGodJazzMedicine: Black Radical Brooklyn*, dotting the neighborhood with four ambitious artworks, including Leigh's homage to Drs. McKinney Steward and English.

The name Free People's Medical Clinic was inspired by the Black Panther Party's Survival programs, which included general health clinics in addition to sickle cell anemia research, free dental care, ambulance services, and optometry programs, among other initiatives.[14] Historian Alondra Nelson wrote about how the Panthers' free-of-charge clinics provided services in neighborhoods often cut off from access and combatted discrimination experienced by patients "who were often relegated to teaching hospitals and their often inexperienced staff." According to Nelson, this is what made the interaction between non-experts working alongside volunteer medical professionals significant. The professionals "trained community health workers to provide basic healthcare. . . . Thus in addition to offering needed treatment, the clinics also embodied the Party's critique of medical authority, professionalization, and the medical-industrial complex.

13
Errol Louis, "Josephine English, One of First Black, Female OB/GYNs, Not Stopping at 89," *New York Daily News*, June 23, 2010, https://www.nydailynews.com/opinion/josephine-english-black-female-ob-gyns-not-stopping-89-article-1.180129.

14
"Program for Survival," *Black Panther*, March 24, 1973, 15, http://www.itsabouttimebpp.com/Survival_Programs/pdf/Survival_Programs.pdf.

15
Alondra Nelson, "The People's Free Medical Clinics," in *Body and Soul: The Black Panther Party and the Fight against Medical Discrimination* (Minneapolis: University of Minnesota Press, 2011), chap. 3, manifold.umn.edu.

16
Rizvana Bradley, "Going Underground: An Interview with Simone Leigh," *Art in America*, August 2015, https://www.artnews.com/art-in-america/interviews/going-underground-an-interview-with-simone-leigh-56438/.

. . . As the Panthers' health work bore out, the Party did not reject medicine outright; rather, it sought to provide and model respectful and reliable medical practice."[15]

Leigh organized her art project around the concept of community care that she saw in these histories, but for legal reasons she was not able to offer actual health services as part of her project. That such barriers emerged in relationship to liability concerns by institutional backers locates the project in a different genre than the outside-the-system work of the Panthers, but this was also a different context and moment in time; such practices have now been taken up by non-profit service providers that did not exist in the days of the Survival programs. Therefore, she focused the project's energy on self-care activities, such as Vinyasa yoga, Black folk dance, black magic, and herbalism; there was also midwifery consultation. Offsite, there was a workshop on Affordable Care Act navigation and free HIV screenings.

As the artist explained in an interview, "The clinic opened in the aftermath of Eric Garner and Michael Brown's deaths that summer. #BlackLivesMatter had emerged as the civil rights movement of our time. Empathy and the lack thereof became a significant recurring idea as I conceived the clinic. Recently multiple studies emerged confirming that both Black and white people, including medical personnel, assume Black people feel less pain than white people."[16] She went on to cite the story of Esmin Elizabeth Green, who died in June 2008 at age forty-nine after waiting twenty-four hours in the psychiatric emergency room of Kings County Hospital in Brooklyn without being seen.

The truth is, as a white cis man, the spaces Leigh created were not intended for me, and so I proceeded into the historic home carefully. I got a partial view of what was happening and that was a real privilege that I could appreciate. But I also knew that I needed to turn around. Poet Tracy K. Smith likens this to the skill of listening in on something that is not for you but that you are implicated in, a skill long honed by people of color but that white people are increasingly asked and invited to develop.[17]

This is not so different from Leigh's 2016 New Museum project *The Waiting Room*, which took institutional resources and dedicated much of the programming to facilitating wellness workshops for young Black women and creating an organizing space that led to, among other activities, the creation of the affinity group Black Women Artists for Black Lives Matter. This group gathered every week for a month for fellowship, sharing art, and conversations about the urgencies of the moment.[18]

This point about gathering in public and naming a specific audience or constituency relates to another historical reference that Leigh has woven into her work: the United Order of Tents, founded in 1867 by Annetta M. Lane and Harriett R. Taylor, who assisted many women escaping slavery via the Underground Railroad and provided care to both enslaved and free Black communities. The United Order of Tents continues to operate today, having maintained throughout its existence a veil of secrecy as to the identity and scope of its work.[19] As curator Helen Molesworth explored in a recent essay, "[I]t's easy to see the parallel [between Leigh and the Tents] . . . because much of Leigh's art is, if not exactly secret, not exactly public, either." She went on to emphasize that Black women are both subject matter and "privileged audience" and that "given the lack of any such systematic inclusion of Black women in the fields of Western culture prior to this moment, this recalibration seems both deeply necessary and positively exhilarating."[20]

Leigh herself framed this position in a social media response to a critic: "I need to say that if you haven't read, not a single thing written by Saidiya Hartman or Hortense Spillers"—and continued here with an incredible enumeration of references to the Black Radical tradition that are embedded in her work at the 2019 Whitney Biennial and elsewhere—"[t]hen you lack the knowledge to recognize the radical gestures in my work. And that is

17
Tracy K. Smith and Michael Kleber-Diggs, "History Is upon Us… Its Hand against Our Back," May 27, 2021, in *On Being with Krista Tippet*, podcast, 50:41, https:// onbeing.org/programs/ tracy-k-smith-and-michael-kleber-diggs-history-is-up-on-us-its-hand-against-our-back/.

18
Jillian Steinhauer, "Reflections from Black Women Artists for Black Lives Matter Avatar," Hyperallergic, September 16, 2016, https://hyperaller-gic.com/322742/reflections-from-black-women-artists-for-black-lives-matter/.

19
Kaitlyn Greenidge, "Secrets of the South," Lenny Letter, 2017, https://www.lennyletter.com/story/secrets-of-the-south.

20
Helen Molesworth, "Underground," *Artforum*, March 2018, https://www.artforum.com/print/201803/helen-molesworth-on-the-work-of-simone-leigh-74304.

21
Simone Leigh, May 16, 2019, on Instagram account of @simoneyvetteleigh, https://www.instagram.com/p/BxiJl58gl4t/.

22
For a discussion of this in relationship to Puerto Rican curators, see Marina Reyes Franco, Thomas Lax, Miguel López, and Thiago de Paula Souza, "Our Island Here: Strategies of Relation in Contemporary Art and Curating," (talk, Program in Latin American Studies and the Department of Art & Archaeology, Princeton University, March 23, 2021), https://vimeo.com/539802787.

23
Sundus Abdul Hadi, *Take Care of Your Self: The Art and Cultures of Care and Liberation* (Brooklyn: Common Notions, 2020), 65.

24
Joshua Bloom and Waldo E. Martin Jr., *Black against Empire: The History and Politics of the Black Panther Party* (Berkeley: University of California Press, 2016), 13.

why, instead of mentioning these things, I have politely said Black women are my primary audience."[21]

It should be clear that this approach demonstrates great care for the audience. While much has been written about the Latin etymology of "curate," meaning to care for, it is typically applied to objects. But, as artists continue to adopt organizing and curatorial tactics, such care extends to both material and "radical care" relationships.[22] Artist and curator Sundus Abdul Hadi promotes the idea of "care-full" curation: "Driven by the people's stories (and their own), many artists have engaged with the concepts of community care and empowerment." She continues, "My hope is that through the care-full curation of art and space, the heavy subjects of trauma, loss, and displacement can transform into opportunities for healing and empowerment."[23]

Deserts and Gardens

Returning to the Panthers' Survival programs, from 1969 through the early 1970s, their Free Breakfast Program and People's Free Food Program were set up in church basements and community centers in cities across the country to feed tens of thousands of hungry kids and adults. In a recent history of the party, authors Joshua Bloom and Waldo E. Martin Jr. proposed that "community programs concretely advanced the politics the Panthers stood for: they were feeding hungry children when the vastly wealthier and more powerful US government was allowing children to starve."[24] They went on to quote FBI Director J. Edgar Hoover in an airtel to the special agent in charge in San Francisco on May 27, 1969: "One of our primary aims in counter-intelligence as it concerns the [party] is to keep this group isolated from the moderate Black and white community which may support it. This is most emphatically pointed out in their Breakfast for Children Program, where they are actively soliciting and receiving

CARE IN CRISIS

support from uninformed whites and moderate blacks."[25] Such cross-racial solidarity continues to be elusive, from politics in general to the specific landscape of food access and, yet, remains a threat to a social hierarchy dependent on racial division.

A major cultural shift in the last decade has been the widespread discussion about food access, an engagement that has led people to classify underserved neighborhoods in American cities as "food deserts" and "food swamps." While those semantic differences have some substance and lead to different characterizations of the situation, the US Department of Agriculture has, as recently as 2015, collected data that estimate 39 million people, or 12.8 percent of the US population, live in "low income and low access areas" or LILAs.[26]

One site of contention in this context is the corner store, or as it is often called in the northeastern US, the bodega, a site where food access could potentially be bridged. These stores make up the majority of food access points in some neighborhoods and tend to sell products that have a longer shelf life, such as sweets and canned goods. In order to combat this, many nonprofit organizations are helping to address store setup costs by buying new refrigeration units for produce and thinking about layouts that maximize space for irregularly shaped products that don't fit on shelves as efficiently as boxes designed for tight packing.[27] The point that is often missed about these corner stores is that, because of the way food distribution works, it is often not economically viable for such businesses to use the distribution systems that supply fresh vegetables. Food distributors frequently have minimum order requirements that are much larger than a corner store can handle. Also, if the smaller stores are even able to access distributors or middlemen, they pay more per unit and, thus, must pass that cost onto their customers.[28]

This leads to often contentious relationships between store owners and their surrounding communities. In urban areas like Philadelphia and Los Angeles, a typical dynamic is that stores are owned

25
Bloom and Martin, *Black against Empire*, 211.

26
"State-Level Estimates of Low Income and Low Access Populations," USDA Food Access Research Atlas, September 30, 2019, https://www.ers.usda.gov/data-products/food-access-research-atlas/state-level-estimates-of-low-income-and-low-access-populations/.

27
Olga Khazan, "Why Convenience Stores Don't Sell Better Food," *Atlantic*, July 2015, https://www.theatlantic.com/politics/archive/2015/07/why-convenience-stores-dont-sell-better-food/432345/.

28
Sam Bloch, "Why Do Corner Stores Struggle to Sell Fresh Produce?," The Counter, February 2019, https://thecounter.org/skid-row-people-market-fresh-affordable-produce-los-angeles/.

29
Kim Jennings, "Korean Liquor Store, Black Neighborhood: A Quarter-Century after the Riots, Misgivings Still Run Deep," *Los Angeles Times*, February 11, 2020, https://www.latimes.com/california/story/2020–02–11/south-los-angeles-korean-liquor-protest-leimert-park-riots.

by Asian immigrants and are located in Black neighborhoods. As a recent *LA Times* story reflected, after a series of incidents at one store in LA owned by Korean Americans in 2017, Black activists organized a boycott of the store, criticizing "the prices a dollar or two higher than at big-box stores, the short treatment from employees who didn't seem to live in or care about the neighborhood, the row of photos taped on the bulletproof glass of suspected shoplifters."[29] And this was not the first time such conflict had occurred. As has been often recounted, during the riots that erupted in South LA after the Rodney King verdict in 1992, over 2,300 Korean-owned businesses were looted and burned.

It was in the aftermath of the LA uprising that Philadelphia's Asian Arts Initiative (AAI) was founded in 1993, with one purpose being to build connections and healing between Asian and Black communities in Philadelphia. Twenty years later, AAI commissioned an art project by Ernel Martinez and Keir Johnson, members of a group of Black and Brown artists called Amber Art and Design, to explore the corner store as a space where Black and Asian communities intersect. Their project investigated "how our relationships are shaped based on which side/s of the counter we may stand [on]," and it involved fabricating phone-booth-sized mobile replicas that resembled cashier counters in corner stores, complete with protective plexiglass. The irresistibly compelling and colorful carts, which could hold one adult comfortably inside, were outfitted with wheels and covered with labels and cartons of products found in such stores, from takeout containers and backlit menus to chip bags and soda bottles. Where the window reveals the torso of the person inside, there was a small countertop and a hole for speaking. The artists pushed the "corner stores," rumbling across the cracked sidewalks over four miles through the city, interacting with takeout restaurants and convenience store owners and customers.

The project, dubbed *Corner Store: Take-Out Stories*, collected input from those witnessing the artists'

CARE IN CRISIS

cross-town trek with the corner store booths. While in motion, they handed out surveys and collected oral histories, and then the results were presented in an exhibition. Workshops were held at AAI with young people whose parents owned stores throughout the city, facilitated by AAI youth programs administrator Ellen Hwang, who actually grew up in the back of her parents' store in the northeast part of the city. Hwang reflected "This is a story from so many immigrants coming to America. They have this American dream idea. . . . They're not only in a place of poverty . . . [but also] the language barrier, the cultural barrier of growing up only around people within your ethnicity and only trusting your own ethnicity, and then coming over here and realizing you don't trust the sound, you don't trust the people."[30]

The members of Amber Art and Design have continued to incorporate food into their work in recent years, often serving meals sourced from neighborhood gardens and chefs. Most recently, they worked with the Rodale Institute in rural Pennsylvania to produce a mural using a soil-science lens to explore urban and rural food connections.

With the emergence of the COVID-19 pandemic, Philadelphia's food insecurity spiked due to changes in store hours and policies; episodes of consumer hoarding; rising food costs amid a massive wave of layoffs and reduced hours; and many populations, particularly the elderly and immunocompromised, simply being unsafe in public spaces with inconsistent physical distancing measures. Concurrently, grocery delivery services boomed in accordance with the parasitic nature of the gig economy. Since the pandemic began, the streets, otherwise quiet due to workplace closures and stay-at-home orders, have been abuzz with doubled-parked delivery drivers.

Numerous religious, social-service, and activist organizations quickly adapted to distribute meals and groceries. At the People's Kitchen—where I worked solidarity shifts during the first year of the pandemic— unemployed chefs, workers, artists, and activists have

30
Cherri Gregg, "New Exhibit Will Take Unique Look at Neighborhood Corner Stores," CBS Local, June 1, 2014, https://philadelphia. cbslocal.com/2014/06/01/ new-exhibit-will-take-unique-look-at-neighbor-hood-corner-stores/. Additional documentation of the project is available at https://vimeo.com/ 97066336.

committed to distributing 215 restaurant-quality hot meals a day. Some groups have opted to fill public refrigerators with free groceries. In a particularly tech-savvy operation that I was involved with in the summer of 2020, a refrigerated warehouse was staffed by unemployed workers for three shifts a day to assemble boxes of donated food. The group was able to make use of a commercial delivery app designed for truckers, which helped volunteers go to a neighborhood pickup site with their deliveries pre-sequenced for the easiest possible movement from home to home. In a weird twist, the logistics revolution that had led to the homogenization of store food shelves has come to aid mutual-aid programs!

Corona Care

Nobody wants to feel useless. Philosopher Donatella Di Cesare has described 2020 as the "anxious existence within the parenthesis," pointing out that the impact it has had on mental health has been tremendous.[31] One question emerging from within the parenthesis is about being useful: about not being useful to exploitative jobs, about jobs that were deemed essential overnight, but also about being useful to the rising tide of justice movements, of being useful toward the self-care or community care.The pandemic has generated a number of new texts with calls for rethinking care, including four from Verso Books alone with titles such as *The Politics of Care: From COVID-19 to Black Lives Matter*; *Care Manifesto: The Politics of Interdependence*; *The Care Crisis: What Caused It and How Can We End It?*; and *Mutual Aid: Building Solidarity During This Crisis (and the Next)*.[32]

Back in the Bronx, Grullón, the artist who had given up counting the unending sirens, was part of a mutual-aid group, the North Bronx Collective, formed along with Vani Kannan, LoriKim Alexander, Lucy Mercado, and Francheska Alcantara. The group started

31
Donatella Di Cesare, *Immunodemocracy: Capitalist Asphyxia* (Cambridge: MIT Press, 2021), 85.

32
Boston Review, ed., *Politics of Care from COVID-19 to Black Lives Matter* (Brooklyn: Verso Books, 2020); The Care Collective, *Care Manifesto: The Politics of Interdependence* (Brooklyn: Verso Books, 2020); Emma Dowling, *The Care Crisis: What Caused It and How Can We End It?* (Brooklyn: Verso Books, 2021); Dean Spade, *Mutual Aid: Building Solidarity during this Crisis (and the Next)* (Brooklyn: Verso Books, 2020).

a food distribution program that was eventually handed off to a local church. They then focused their energy on restoring, remediating, and starting to garden in a disinvested area owned by the park district, which Grullón has been involved with for several years.[33] Anecdotally, this kind of engagement in mutual aid by artists seemed to blossom widely—which could be read, depending on who you ask, as adding an increased centrality of activism to today's art activism, or conversely, as meaning that that artists might be inclined to make greater distinctions between what constitutes solidarity and what constitutes their art.

At the start of the pandemic, Grullón began a new series of self-portrait photographs produced in her home, where she was quarantining. In the series March to June: At Home with Essential Workers (2020), the title of each work includes the date when it was taken and a hyperlink to a picture of the essential worker whom Grullón dresses as in the portrait. For instance, there is *March 31, 2020: Rikers Island Prisoners Are Being Offered PPE and $6 an Hour to Dig Mass Graves https://theintercept.com/2020/03/31/rikers-island-coronavirus-mass-graves/*, in which the artist stands, barefoot, in what appears to be a household entryway or hallway, wearing an orange prison jumpsuit, her arms hanging at her side and gaze looking slightly to the right of the camera, while to her left hangs a chandelier with some missing bulbs. And then there is *April 28, 2020: As Amazon, Walmart, and Others Profit amid Coronavirus Crisis, Their Essential Workers Plan Unprecedented Strike—https://theintercept.com/2020/04/28/coronavirus-may-1-strike-sickout-amazon-target-whole-foods/*. In this image, the artist mounts a bicycle, a helmet and a bag hanging over the handlebars, again with her gaze directed at the camera, her facemask hanging below her nose but covering her mouth. This time, the setting is a kitchen, complete with dishes in a dish rack and a microwave in the background.[34]

Rather than oscillating between private and public, the images hold both spheres in the same

33
Hakim Bishara, "Bronx Artists Collaborated to Refurbish Community Park until the City Locked Them Out," Hyperallergic, April 6, 2021, https://hyperallergic.com/632855/north-bronx-collective-refurbish-tibbetts-tail-nyc-parks-locked-out/. See also North Bronx Collective, "Why NYC Mutual Aid Workers Are Cutting Ties with World Central Kitchen," Medium, June 18, 2020, https://medium.com/@northbronxmutualaid/why-nyc-mutual-aid-workers-are-cutting-ties-with-world-central-kitchen-335cfec40189; and North Bronx Collective, "Hot City: Reimagining Food Justice in an Uprising," *Verso Books Hot City* (blog), October 14, 2020, https://www.versobooks.com/blogs/4875-hot-city-re-imagining-food-jus-tice-in-an-uprising.

34
Alicia Grullón, March to June: At Home with Essential Workers, online exhibition, July 23–November 23, 2020, Bronx Museum of the Arts, 2020, http://www.bronxmuseum.org/index.php/exhibitions/alicia-grullon-march-to-june-at-home-with-essential-workers-online-exhibition.

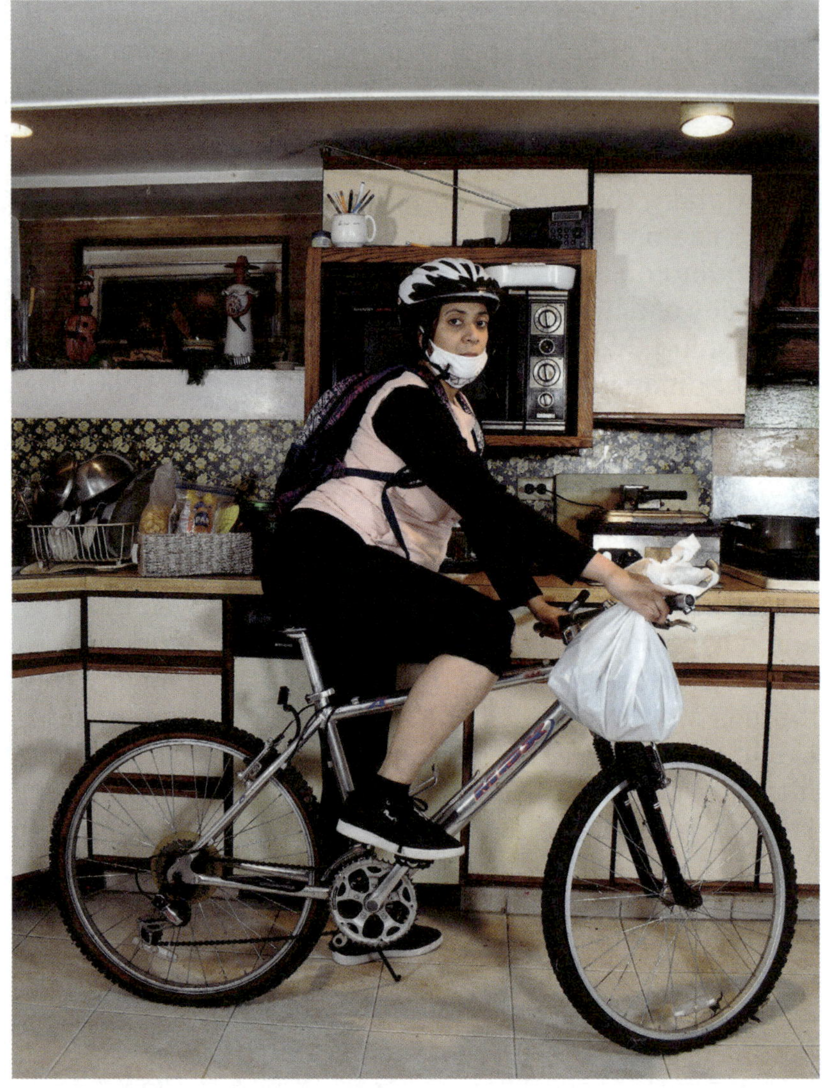

photograph. One figure is depicted simultaneously as an iconic essential worker who is transported from their workplace to a personal, domestic space. The URLs and article headlines incorporated into the titles of the artworks add an additional register, that of media representation and dissemination, where the reported narratives offer context. In these images, Grullón *becomes* the essential workers outside—a postal worker, food delivery person, and a nurse—in an act of empathy, but she also remains physically distanced inside her

CARE IN CRISIS

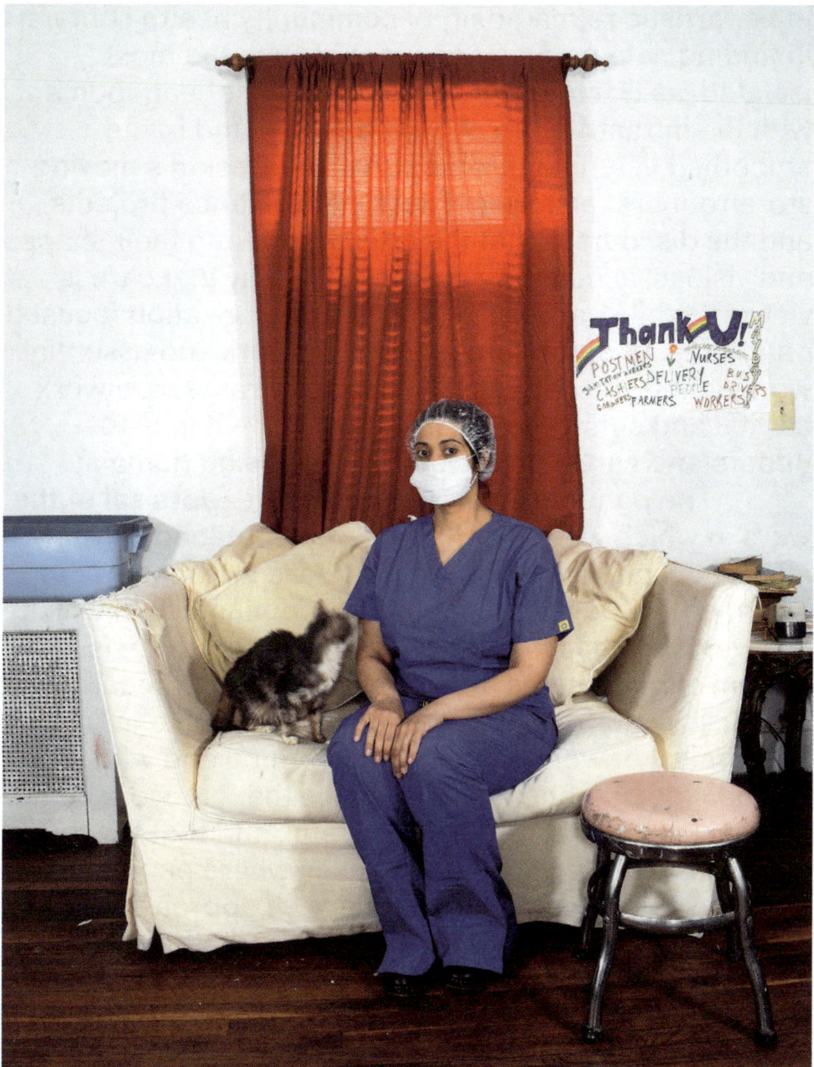

Alicia Grullón, *April 13, 2020: NYC Death Toll Jumps by 3,700 after Uncounted Fatalities Are Added, https:// www. politico.com/states/ new-york/albany/story/ 2020/04/14/new-york-city-coronavirus-death-toll-jumps-by-3-700-after-un-counted-fatalities-are-add-ed-1275931*, 2020. Archival color dye sublimation print on aluminum, 40 × 60 inches. Courtesy of the artist.

own home in an act of solidarity. These aesthetic choices say a lot about the artist's analysis of the interconnectedness of struggles, and, also reflect the practical parameters of a pandemic lockdown.

To the extent that a defining characteristic of the pandemic-era artwork may be emerging, it can be directly connected to the politics of care. Building upon previous work that was already exploring care even before the pandemic, I suspect it will continue to be about excavating important histories, as Leigh took up in her artistic reimagining of community health centers; in finding safe points of connection with the most isolated, as Basting proposed through her engagement with the infrastructure of food delivery; and in the embodied listening of Amber Art and Design's moving storefront oral histories. These performance projects, and the discourses that the artists wove into their shapes and visions, account for a shift in the way that care is viewed. While earlier advocacy and theorization focused on valuing all of the things that care work and essential work enable, there is now a push to reframe care work as vital and central to the meaning of life itself—to understand care work as the work of being human.

The pandemic has promoted a reappraisal of the ways in which we live. It has led to heightened scrutiny about how public health systems have historically informed the development of the communities in which we live, and it has made clear that this largely invisible system of institutions and infrastructures is precarious and disinvested. The pandemic has also led to a reappraisal of work, about what is valued and who is valued. Looking ahead, the premise that our work could be seen and valued as socially useful, and that the towns and cities we live in could be places where people feel safe and cared for must guide how we approach public policies, as well as the ways in which we simply relate to one another. The aesthetic, social, and political experiments of this moment will undoubtedly have lasting effects on what art and activism look like moving forward, so let's give them the care they deserve now. Our future will be better for it.

BREAKING DOWN TO BUILD UP: *A Cultural Emergency Response*

Erin Genia

We are now living through a vast array of interconnected and existential crises. Climate change, institutional racism, economic inequality, ecological collapse, a global pandemic, Indigenous peoples' dispossession, and so many others threaten not only the lives and livelihoods of people across a multiplicity of divides, but also the future survival of our species and the web of life on Earth. How are we to understand the level of emergency we find ourselves in, and what can we do about it?

Current political, economic, and social attempts to address these crises fall short, and the most important causative factor remains unacknowledged: they are rooted in our cultural practices. In all sectors of our society, the evidence that we are in a state of cultural emergency is mounting, and people are demanding and organizing for change. Yet our culture seems incapable of altering its trajectory without the impetus of mass movements, war, or large-scale disruptions.

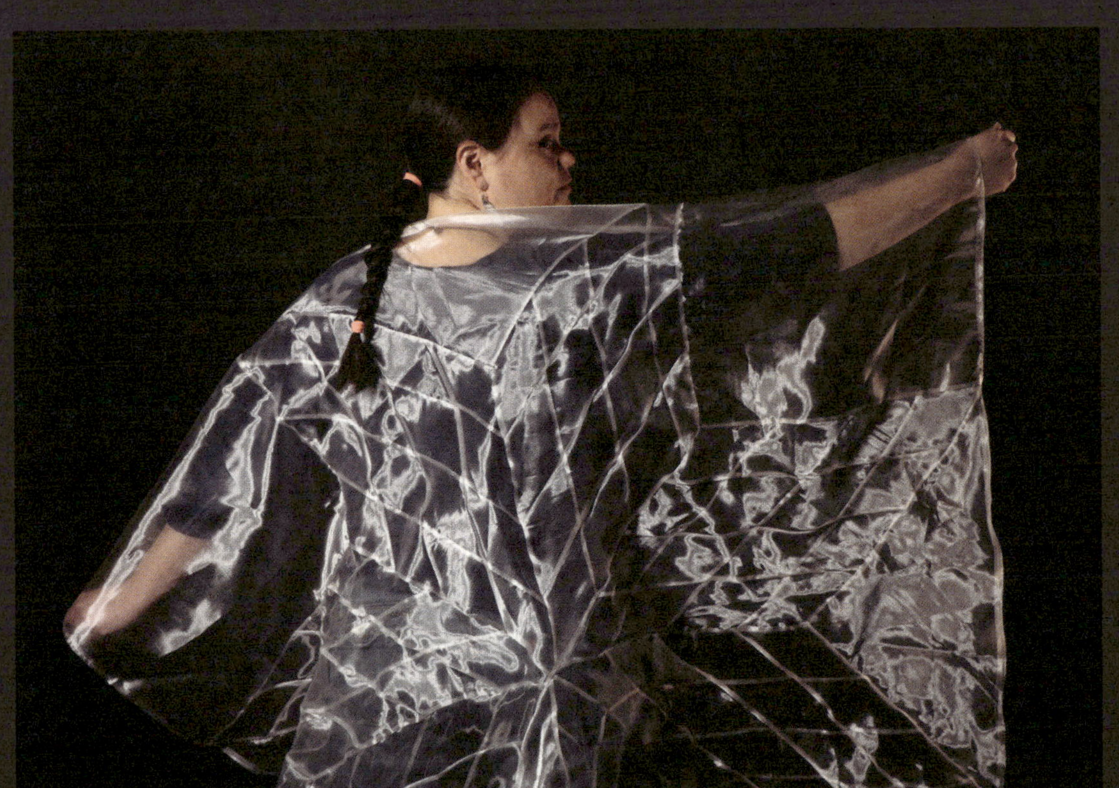

BREAKING DOWN TO BUILD UP

InVisible, 2017

When worn as a shawl, *InVisible* provides a symbolic
skin of protection against pervasive cultural supremacy.
The morningstar form is an expression of cultural
power, which is used here to transform. Is white cultural
supremacy, which expropriates and erases other
cultures, a translucent veil so pervasive that it's
imperceptible to those living under it? As a Dakota
person, I experience cultural supremacy as a tool of the
dominant culture, which sets itself as the standard,
forces assimilation, and constantly perpetuates itself to
reinforce structures and institutions that maintain a
limited picture of reality. The white gossamer fabric of
this shawl is nearly transparent, but, as it moves, it
reflects rays of light in a full spectrum of colors, affirming
its self-possessed strength of presence. It is a reminder
that other realities are possible.

A historical perspective shows that our society has always been on a self-destructive path because the philosophies and ideologies that undergird its progress are profoundly misaligned with the natural world, and therefore the basis of all life. This has created a fundamental imbalance that constantly seeks equilibrium through the expropriation of the lives, lands, labors, and cultures of those outside of its bounds. The pattern of harm began with Western European imperialism—rooted in the Roman empire—and spread across the globe through colonization, the global slave trade, and neoliberal capitalism. As a result, communities across the world are in various states of chaos, conflict, misery, and ecological degradation. This legacy continues to mutate and expand, unabated, so it is only natural that we find ourselves in a state of emergency. It is imperative that we understand this. No solutions will be effective that do not implicate our society's cultural norms and strategize to remedy them at every level.

Due to the extreme level of crisis we find ourselves in, scholars, artists, leaders, scientists, and others operating within the Western cultural framework may feel tempted to expropriate from Indigenous peoples' knowledges, which are currently hailed as "new ways of thinking" and pursued as the latest trend for seeking to balance Western praxis, which is essentially irredeemable. Indigenous peoples' properties have always been seen and used as a solution to whatever crises Western systems have faced throughout their centuries-long tenure of dominance. Modernism, a foundation of present-day art, design, and philosophical practices, is a good example of this extractive tendency.

My life experience has given me the perspective to see the deep harms caused by American institutions and systems because I exist simultaneously inside and outside of American culture and hail from Indigenous peoples—Dakota and Odawa—who have been targeted for destruction by the dominant culture for hundreds of years. As an artist and community organizer, I believe these harms should not be tolerated as inevitable or acceptable. If we are serious about solutions beyond superficial fixes, then we must collectively conduct concerted, system-wide examinations of how American culture produces them so that we can end them.

During my artist residency with the City of Boston's Office of Emergency Management, I developed the Cultural Emergency Response framework as a way to advocate for a major shift in our collective approaches to solving the most pressing crises of our times. The framework creatively repurposes disaster management methods and materials to address emergencies' root causes. This work came about, in part, through public community conversations surrounding public art, monuments, and commemorative landscapes organized over the past year. The first was a three-panel virtual series entitled Confronting Colonial Myths in Boston's Public Space, in which Indigenous leaders, artists, and allies spoke about how symbols perpetuating colonial myths affect the lives of Indigenous people in the city and contribute to the public health emergency of racism.[1] This was followed by Centering Justice: Indigenous Artists' Perspectives on Public Art, a multi-day virtual symposium and a series of articles published on the public art blog of the New England Foundation for the Arts.[2] Centering Justice presented critical perspectives on the intertwined economic, ecological, cultural, and social justice dimensions of public space in order to disrupt harmful historic narratives, interrogate the ongoing legacy and impacts of settler colonization, address Indigenous peoples' ongoing invisibility in the public sphere, and generate momentum toward increased understanding to spark vital transformational change.

A State of Cultural Emergency

A cultural emergency is a convergence of urgent, widespread crises that stem from the cultural practices of our society. The ideologies and philosophies that drive culture determine how our economic, political, and

[1]
ERIN GENIA: Boston Artist-in-Residence," City of Boston, https://www.boston.gov/departments/arts-and-culture/erin-genia

[2]
New England Foundation for the Arts (website), "Centering Justice: Indigenous Artists' Perspectives on Public Art," https://www.nefa.org/CenteringJustice

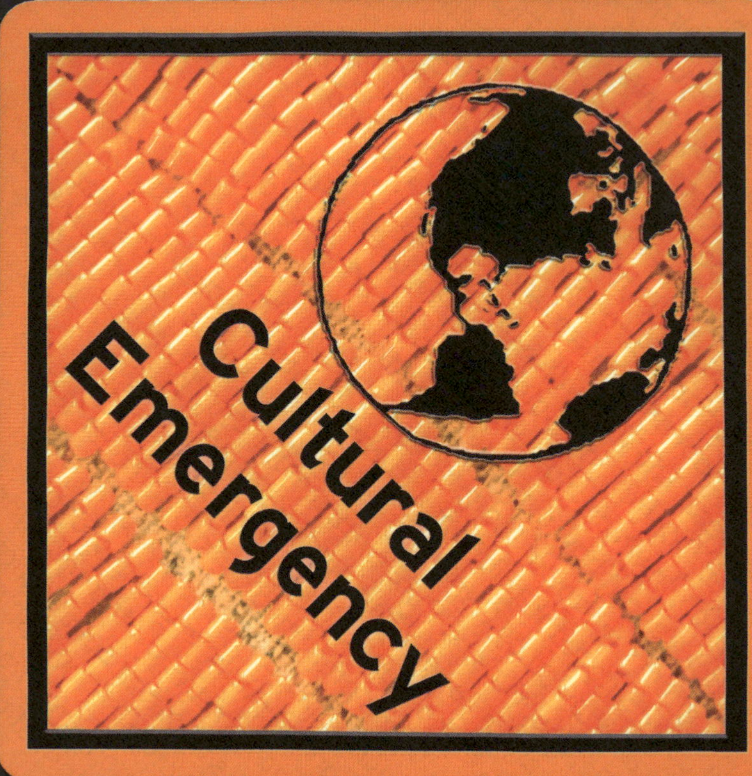
Cultural
Emergency

BREAKING DOWN TO BUILD UP

Cultural Emergency Response, 2020–2021

Climate change, institutional racism, economic inequality, ecological destruction, and Indigenous peoples' dispossession are among the most pressing issues of our time. Their root causes stem from the philosophies embedded within dominant cultural practices. In order to adequately attend to these difficult and interconnected problems, we must look to their origins. As a 2020-2021 artist in residence for the City of Boston's Office of Emergency Management, I developed *Cultural Emergency Response* as a framework for understanding how the field of Emergency Management can be leveraged to create responses to societal crises at a cultural level.[1]

By declaring a state of cultural emergency, we can see how major emergencies are inseparable from the cultural tenets that produce them and envision how the tools and techniques of emergency management can be used to respond to them. Emergency management planning methods used by local, state, federal and tribal agencies work are coordinated across many agencies and organizations to address serious logistical problems and save lives. Careful planning, strategizing, and budgeting—as well as the consideration of contingencies—help to develop potential responses to disaster incidents like floods, storms, chemical spills, rioting, and pandemics. All of the necessary resources, people and institutions are marshalled to rapidly respond before, during, and after an emergency. These are the kinds of efforts that are needed to address the root cultural causes of major societal emergencies.

1

"Cultural Emergency Response," City of Boston, accessed September 24, 2021, https://www.boston.gov/cultural-emergency.

social systems are established and how they operate.
We take for granted that the same doctrines we subscribe
to, and rely on, to fuel societal progress simultaneously
result in extensive disaster situations. Without correcting
course, the harmful byproducts of our culture accumulate
in urgency and scale. Cultural emergencies can be
both acute and chronic, often developing over a long
period of time to reach a critical state. They are often
interconnected, affect diverse peoples, compound social
disparities, and limit collective resiliency.

Some examples of the harmful byproducts of our
culture are:

- climate change
- institutionalized racism and white supremacy
- environmental catastrophes from resource
  extraction
- mass extinctions
- extreme political polarization
- global war, militarism, and the possibility of
  nuclear annihilation
- genocide, apartheid, and colonization
- slavery, human trafficking, and incarceration
- technologies divorced from natural world–
  based wisdom
- extreme wealth hoarding and poverty
- pandemics and other epidemics

As a cultural worker who is active within social movements
that hold institutions and systems accountable, I have
worked on many of these issues, and yet I have found
few mechanisms that address their root cultural causes—
and no common language or underlying framework to
undertake this task. Identifying how our cultural norms
produce harmful byproducts and reckoning with
the history that created our current state of crisis are
essential first steps towards this goal.

The United States has a long and ongoing record
of causing trauma to Indigenous people and those

whom it marginalizes within and outside of its borders. The ideologies that drove its founding as a settler-colonial state, built its economic wealth, and advanced its political power through genocide, land theft, slavery, and war have remained pervasive. They emerged from imperial Western epistemologies, which I loosely and inclusively define as a legacy built from Indo-European, Greco-Roman, and Judeo-Christian cultures. The doctrines fueling the cultural practices that enable these harms began long before settlers came to this continent and have continued to intensify over many generations. Consequently, every person in our society has been indoctrinated into perpetuating cultural harm on some level. It is therefore incumbent upon each person to own their position in this state of cultural emergency and take necessary action.

Culture begins with behaviors that are embedded in the rituals of daily life. In order to survive, the reality is that people orient themselves toward systems that create harmful byproducts. It is possible to acknowledge the challenges of this dynamic and be critical about how to position ourselves based upon our own unique situations. Because cultural practices are deeply internalized, it can be difficult to let go of them—no matter how harmful they may be. As we hold our institutions accountable, we must also hold our communities and ourselves accountable.

From my perspective as a Sisseton-Wahpeton Oyate tribal member, I see the ways in which Western thought holds sway over the thinking, imaginations, practices, and policies of people belonging to the dominant culture. It is so profoundly embedded in the issues we face that it has become hard to see as the root problem. I have been thinking about this for a long time and have identified the following harmful philosophical constructs that are present in Western thought and inform American culture:

- toxic individuality and separation from the natural world and others
- hierarchical thinking, binary thinking,

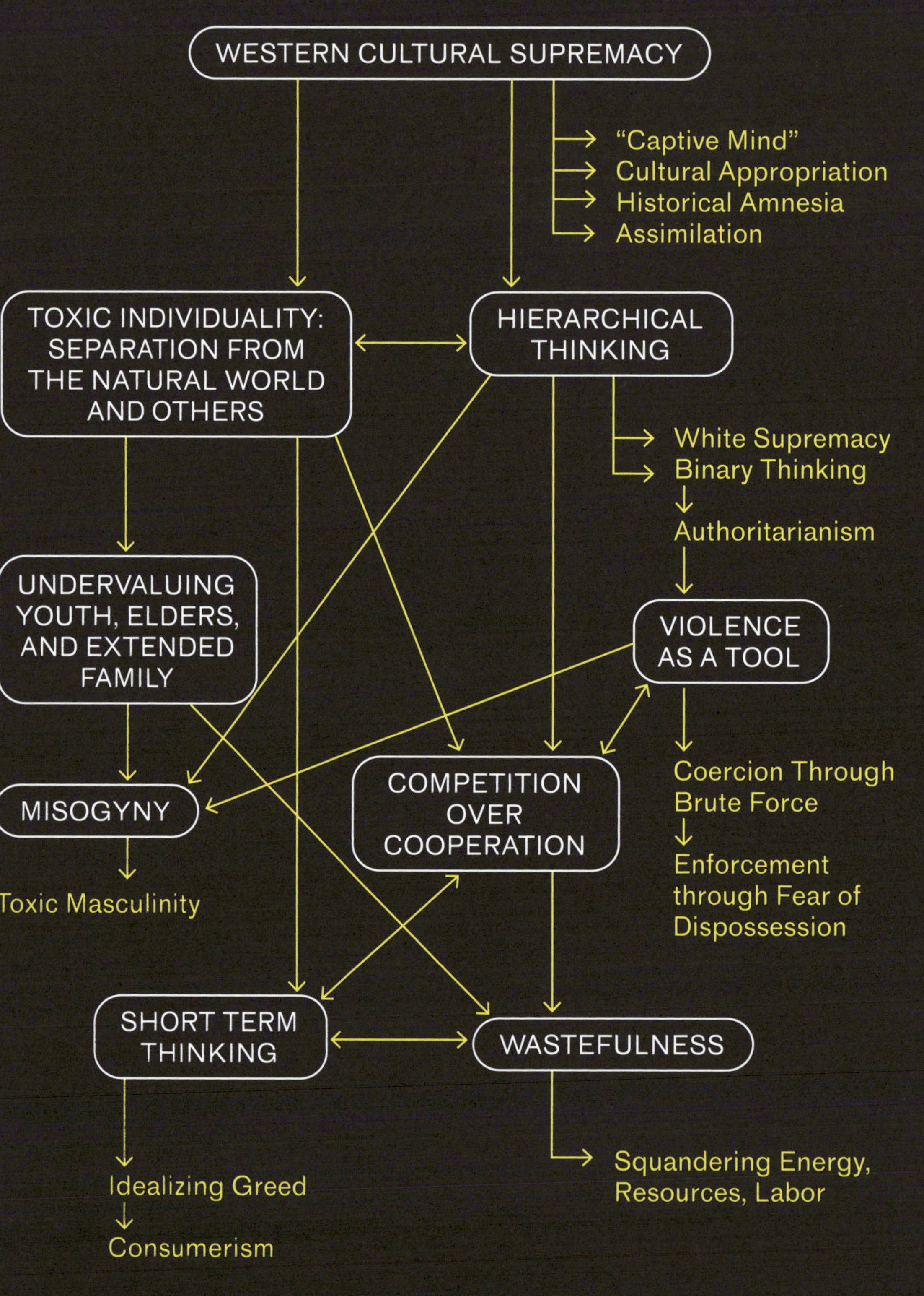

WESTERN CULTURAL SUPREMACY
"Captive Mind"
Cultural Appropriation
Historical Amnesia
Assimilation
TOXIC INDIVIDUALITY: SEPARATION FROM THE NATURAL WORLD AND OTHERS
HIERARCHICAL THINKING
White Supremacy
Binary Thinking
Authoritarianism
UNDERVALUING YOUTH, ELDERS, AND EXTENDED FAMILY
VIOLENCE AS A TOOL
Coercion Through Brute Force
Enforcement through Fear of Dispossession
MISOGYNY
COMPETITION OVER COOPERATION
Toxic Masculinity
SHORT TERM THINKING
WASTEFULNESS
Idealizing Greed
Squandering Energy, Resources, Labor
Consumerism

What are the ways of thinking and acting within our culture that create emergencies and cause harm? This is neither an exhaustive list nor a definitive map, but a sketch of overarching concepts and possible connections. More work must be done in community to identify harmful cultural constructs.

Erin Genia

3
Malaysian scholar and statesman Syed Hussein Alatas said that a "captive mind" "is the product of higher institutions of learning, either at home or abroad, whose way of thinking is dominated by Western thought in an imitative and uncritical manner." It is "uncreative and incapable of raising original problems," "incapable of devising an analytical method independent of current stereotypes," and "incapable of separating the particular from the universal in science and thereby properly adapting the universally valid corpus of scientific knowledge to the particular local situations." Further, a mind "fragmented in outlook," was, for him, "alienated from the major issues of society"; "alienated from its own national tradition, if it exists, in the field of its intellectual pursuit"; "unconscious of its own captivity and the conditioning factors making it what it is"; "not amenable to an adequate quantitative analysis but it can be studied by empirical observation"; and "a result of the Western dominance over the rest of the world." Syed Hussein Alatas, "The Captive Mind and Creative Development," in *Indigeneity and Universality in Social Science: A South Asian Response*, ed. Partha N. Mukherji and Chandan Sengupta (New York: Sage Publications, 2004), 83.

and authoritarianism
- misogyny and toxic masculinity
- short-term thinking and historical amnesia
- idealizing greed and consumerism
- violence as a tool, coercion through brute force, and fear of dispossession
- Western cultural supremacy and assimilation
- the "captive mind"[3]
- competition over cooperation
- wastefulness and the squandering of energy, resources, and labor
- cultural appropriation
- undervaluing youth, elders, and the extended family

This list is not comprehensive; rather it is a sketch of ideological attributes that contribute to cultural emergencies and indicates where more consideration is warranted. We can evolve beyond these if we recognize our mistakes, learn from them, and then change course and move forward.

Addressing the cultural emergencies that are the most pressing issues of our time will require reworking and rethinking the systems that contribute to them. A cultural emergency response can guide us to a more widespread, grassroots cultural change that is required of this moment by bringing together movements, leaders, scholars, artists, community workers, agencies and organizations who have done the work of proposing and enacting solutions to major societal issues. Disaster management strategies provide powerful models and tools for directing resources, streamlining processes, providing support networks, and creating road maps to address cultural emergencies that reflect unique community needs.

Cultural Supremacy and Indigenous Peoples' Dispossession

A powerful impediment to this work is the extreme cultural supremacy inherent in Western praxis. Countless platforms, discourses, and media incessantly privilege its philosophies as superior, despite its dubious legacy. This cultural supremacy is bound up with assimilationist and appropriative practices enabled by the violence and subjugation it has wrought to gain dominance around the world. The repercussions of centuries of its anti-Indigenous imperial warfare and killing and enslaving people on a massive scale have resulted in the destruction of Earth-based cultures across the globe. Its trajectory leads the way forward, from one disaster to another.

It is in these times of crises—when allegiance to the hyper-individualistic, hierarchical, and linear characteristics of Western culture cannot be reconciled with natural law—that its adherents seek harmony by looking beyond its boundaries. Rather than confront the defective reasoning at its foundation, a common practice is to supplement its philosophical shortcomings with new or "other" ways of thinking. The dissonance between Indigenous peoples' thoughts, cultures, and ways and those of Western culture is a source of fascination that leads to exploitation.

As a Dakota person, I witness how the concepts that form the basis of Dakota culture appear new, liberatory, or reparative to those steeped in Western methodologies. Expropriating from Indigenous cultures is currently in vogue across art and science disciplines, but this is neither new nor innovative. Our cultures, lands, lives, and properties are, and have always been, sought-after objects of desire within the dominant culture. Western thought follows trends, repudiating past ideas in favor of novel ones. Indigenous culture is today's latest frontier to hunt, obtain, use, and then inevitably discard.

Such expropriation manifests in the art world with artists in each succeeding generation who reject the

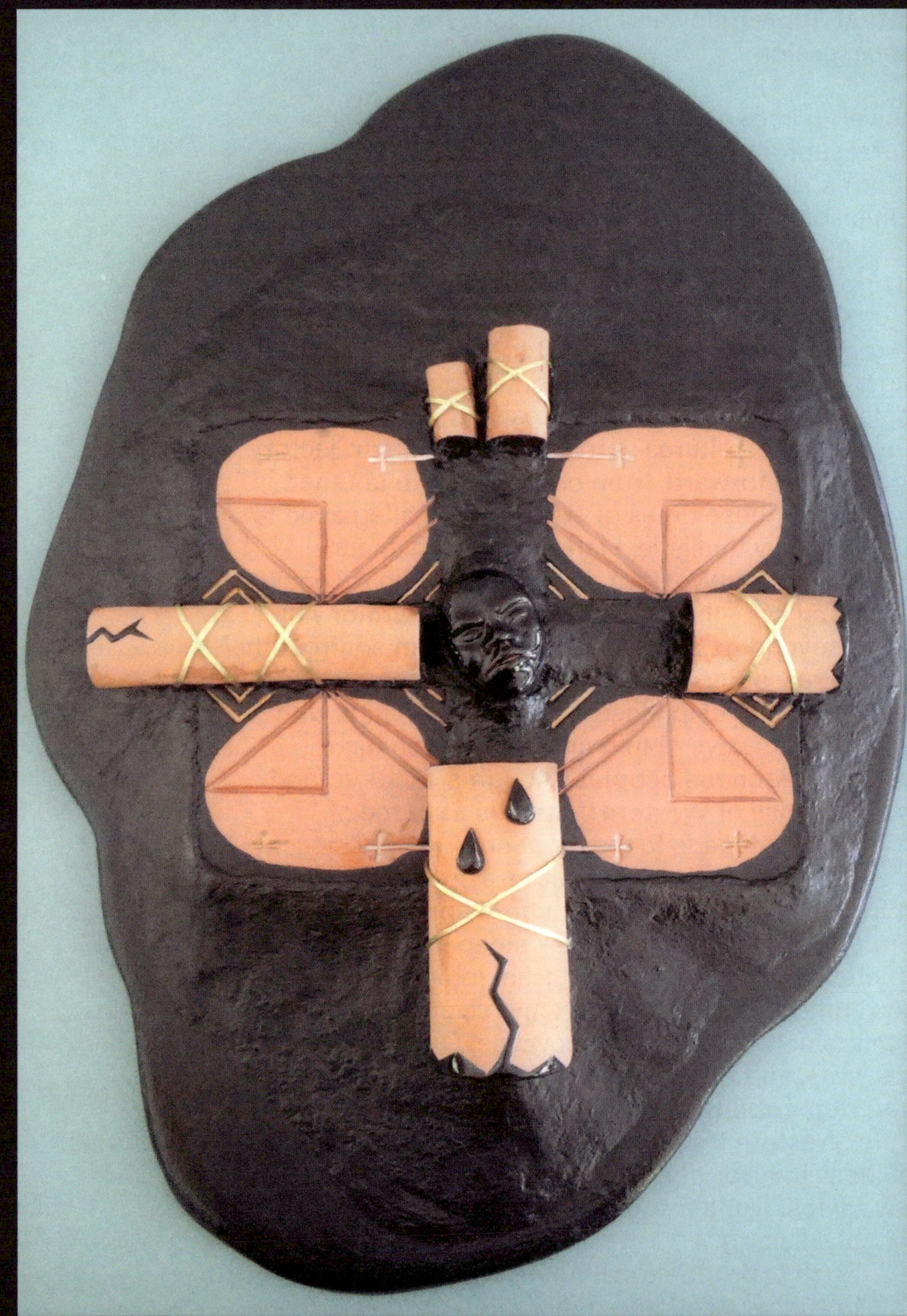

BREAKING DOWN TO BUILD UP

Facing/Not Facing: Toxic Devastation from Oil, 2016

Broken pipelines delineate the four directions, the spill reaches out to all corners of the Earth. At the heart of the crisis are humans, who are both responsible for this and endangered by it.

The Standing Rock Sioux Tribe—backed by every other tribe within the Očeti Sakowin/Great Sioux Nation, along with people from tribes all over the globe and non-Indigenous allies worldwide—fought to protect the Missouri River Basin, tribal lands, and sacred sites from invasion by the Dakota Access Pipeline and won.

The #NoDAPL struggle came at a crucial time in our collective present: energy extraction industries, empowered by government institutions, are destroying our environment to the detriment of our survival as a species and the entire web of life. This is a battle that the people are fighting with nonviolent means and spiritual power against the destructive and corrupt forces waging a war on the Earth. Violence as a tactic against our people will not work in this long-term struggle. For too long, Indigenous peoples have endured the brunt of environmental racism. Might does not make right, despite the show of power that American forces (military, police, agencies, and corporations) have used to impose their will and to subdue people they deem as lesser, or as a threat to their profits. The #NoDAPL movement brought forth the necessary voices of Indigenous peoples, which America and other colonizing powers have tried to silence for hundreds of years. Without our voices, the world is out of balance. Indigenous peoples and cultures are essential to the human family and the world. We demand the respect we deserve, beginning with free, prior, and informed consent.

Erin Genia

creative practices and thinking of the past generation in favor of something new. This is different from the orientation of Dakota art and creative practices, which build upon the lessons and wisdom of our ancestors and do not view the past as something to rebuke.

Dakota ways of knowing and understanding have long been demeaned and used to discredit us in order to validate our dispossession and the genocide of our people. These ways have been targeted for erasure by US assimilation policies, which have been carried out through forcible indoctrination at boarding schools and the destruction of tribal political and economic systems. However, colonialism has not been successful in eliminating us; we have maintained our ways in the face of centuries of ethnic cleansing and land loss, and we continue to resist the policies that are aimed at absorbing us into the behemoth of Western culture. Resistance to assimilation and cultural appropriation are necessary to preserving, maintaining, and creating the conditions for cultural growth and well-being.

This effort is both arduous and constant because cultural appropriation is indispensable to Western expansionism. Like breathing, this appropriation is an automatic reflex by members of the dominant culture. Its defenders argue that it represents cultural sharing. But sharing implies that each party is on equal footing, with an equal distribution of goodwill, and the power dynamic between Indigenous peoples and settlers is marked by inequality and discord. Indigenous tribes are in a state of prolonged occupation in the US, and there can be no sharing of culture when one people is subjugated by another.

A major example of the way in which cultural appropriation influences present-day creative practices can be found in modernism. One of the most influential movements in Western art and culture, it originated at a time when European and American societies were facing the cultural emergencies of war, totalitarianism, and economic inequality alongside rapid developments in technology. Shaped by colonialist values, the gaze of primitivism, and cultural supremacy, the modernists expropriated Indigenous, African, and other non-Western peoples' cultural practices and design principles to incorporate them into their creative forms. This practice shaped a new generation of aesthetic conventions and theoretical faiths, while at the same time genocide and colonization were actively dispossessing the progenitors of the sought-after knowledge. Without transparency regarding its complicity in the deprivation of the people who were its sources of inspiration, modernism contributed to the demand for stolen Indigenous artifacts, fueled false narratives of authenticity and cultural purity, and cemented cultural appropriation as a design practice that Indigenous peoples must contend with to this day.

There is an intellectual tradition among those who see the injustices of Western epistemology and speak out and work against it. Historian and thinker Howard Zinn, for instance, wrote in his book *Artists in Times of War*:

> So, the word transcendent comes to mind when I think of the role of the artist in dealing with the issues of the day. I use the word to suggest that the role of the artist is to transcend conventional wisdom, to transcend the word for the establishment, to transcend the orthodoxy, to go beyond or escape what is handed down by the government or what is said in the media... It is the job of the artist to transcend that—to think outside the boundaries of permissible thought and dare say the things no one else will say.[4]

Artists and thinkers who understand that the philosophies underlying the Western canon are fundamentally flawed have grappled with its shortcomings. In 1972, Hungarian artist György Kepes wrote:

> Disregard for nature's richness leads to the destruction of living forms and eventually to

4
Howard Zinn, *Artists in Times of War* (New York: Seven Stories Press, 2003), 1–4.

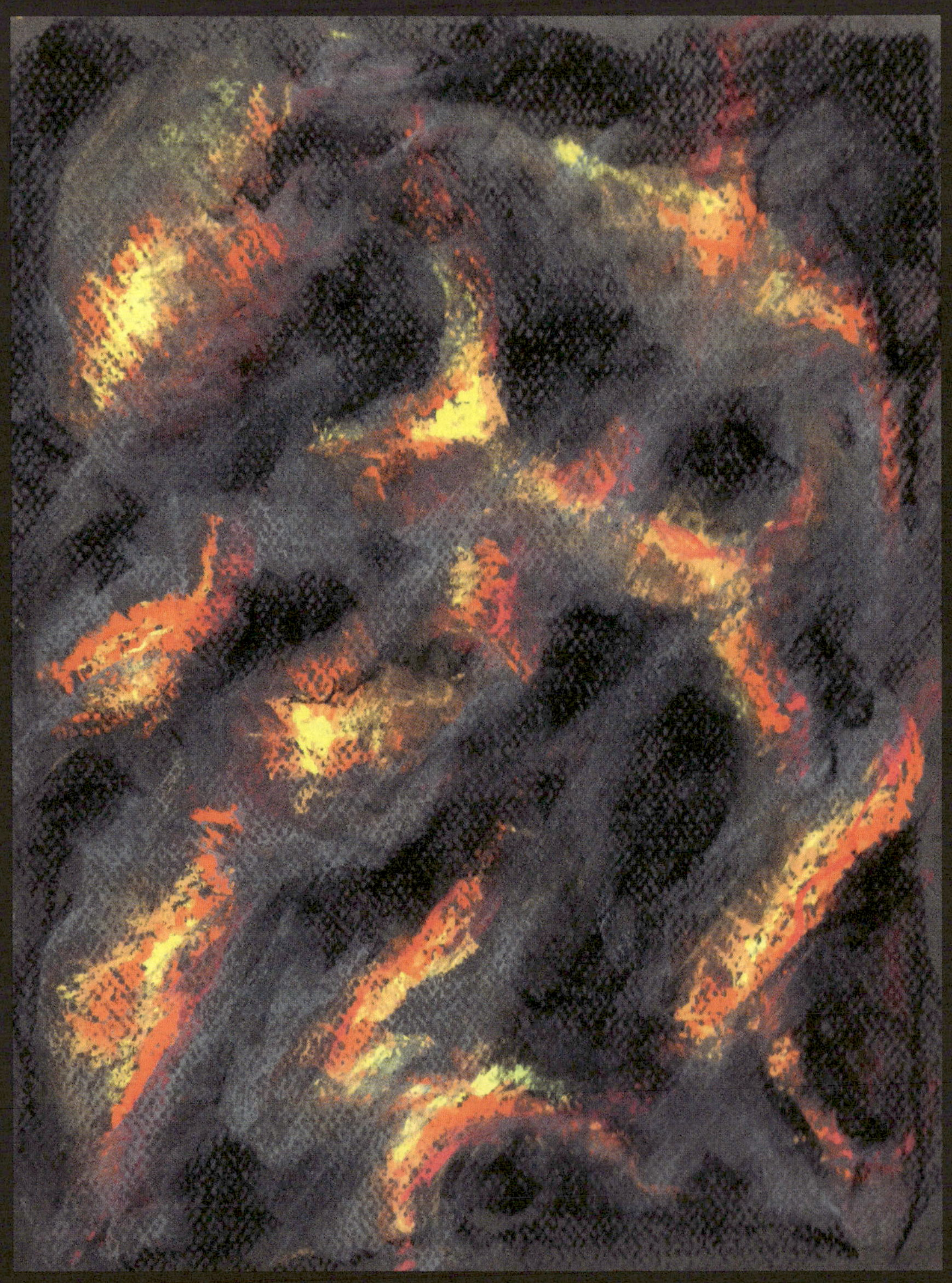

BREAKING DOWN TO BUILD UP

Colonial Legacy: Uncontrolled Burn, 2018

The work depicts a wildfire from above. The increasing
number and severity of forest fires stem from the
colonial legacy of destroying Earth-based ways of
knowing that are carried by Indigenous peoples. One of
these ways of knowing is the centuries-old practice
of stewarding landscapes through a variety of methods,
including controlled burns to manage forests. The loss
of Indigenous peoples practicing these methods over
widespread areas, accompanied by the prevalent view
that the natural world is a set of resources meant for
human and industrial consumption alone, has inevitably
led to ecosystemic collapse and climate change.

Erin Genia

the degradation and destruction of man himself. And although an increasing number of people realize the urgent need for change, we are all carried along by the uncontrolled dynamic of our situation and continue to develop ever more powerful tools without a code of values to guide their use.[5]

In the same work, *Art and Ecological Consciousness*, he discusses the role of the artist and the potential for art to be a site of fertile inquiry into these failings:

> A cornered man is compelled to look into himself and gauge his own strengths and weaknesses. He must examine closely the nature of his relationship with his fellow man and with the world. Our unresolved and troubled lives compel us to reassess ourselves, and nowhere is our questioning of goals and means more evident than in the visual arts. Perhaps these responses can indicate what went wrong and where we should look for answers.[6]

Artists and creatives who prize freedom of thought and freedom of expression are not exempt from the reality that they are operating within a power dynamic that is dependent on the dispossession of Indigenous people and the labor, lands, and lives of others. The field of art is an arena where fallacies can be challenged, and yet, without a commitment to doing that by decolonizing culture, there can be no real progress. As Vine Deloria Jr. wrote, "The imminent and expected destruction of the life cycle of world ecology can be prevented by a radical shift in outlook from our present naive conception of this world as a testing ground of abstract morality to a more mature view of the universe as a comprehensive matrix of life forms."[7] It should be obvious that listening to Indigenous peoples rather than taking from us is a good place to start.

5
György Kepes, "Art and Ecological Consciousness," in *Arts of the Environment,* Vision Value Series (New York: G. Braziller, 1972), 2.

6
Kepes, "Art and Ecological Consciousness," 5

7
Vine Deloria Jr., *God Is Red,* 3rd ed. (Golden, CO: Fulcrum Publishing, 2003), 288.

When all is said and done, continuing along the same path will not lead to a different result, it will only deepen our state of cultural emergency. Instead of attempting to redeem Western approaches, we must begin by thoroughly examining the artifice inherent in Western praxis through clarity of thought, just systems development, and place- and community-based methodologies. Fostering actual innovation through the creative process is an avenue of redress, criticality, inspiration, and realization to move us forward together. Ultimately, each person is responsible for repairing, replacing, and creating the culture we share. We must break it down to build it up.

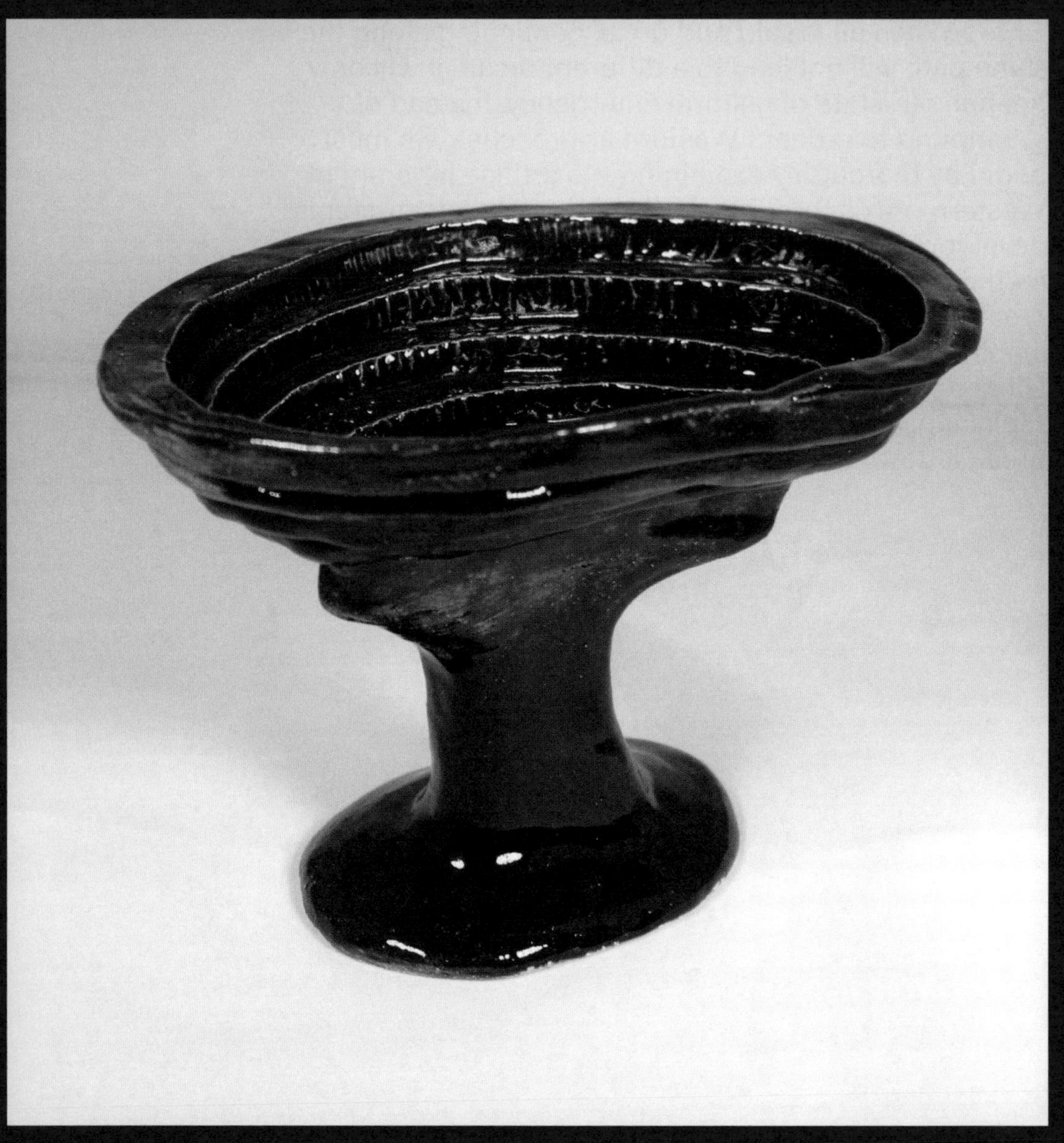

Iȟpéya/Piyéhpičašni: Midnight Mine Goblet, **2018**

Once the sought-after parts of the Earth's body are taken and processed into the "essential elements that make modern living possible,"[1] what happens to the landscapes left behind?

In the Dakhota language, Iȟpéyá means to discard/throw away, and it is used here to describe the increasing number of places on Earth that are spent, trashed, contaminated, detonated, and destroyed. Piyéhpičašni means broken beyond repair/unfixable, and, in this context, it implicates Western philosophies of separation from nature and the hierarchy of man, which, compounded over hundreds of years of dominance, have caused widespread ecological collapse and climate change.

Dakota philosophy holds that humans are not separate from or greater than the Earth and its processes. With this in mind, how can we attend to the drastically changed landscapes resulting from widespread human-caused environmental degradation? Uranium from Midnite Mine on the Spokane Indian Reservation in Washington helped to fuel the Cold War, and the mine is now a Superfund site. We don't have to look far to see landscapes altered by modern living. What's harder to see is the imperative of remembering our deep relationship to the land we live on/land we are.

1
"At Rio Tinto Kennecott, We Mine Essential Elements that Make Modern Living Possible . . . Nearly Everything Used Today Relies on Materials We Produce," Rio Tinto Kennecott (website), accessed September 24, 2021, http://www.kennecott.com/about-us.

AN ECOLOGY OF ARRANGEMENTS:
An Interview with Design Studio for Social Intervention

Anthony Romero

> We assert that now is a critical time to focus our collective attention on the global and local arrangements implicated in the management of the coronavirus. We want folks who care about social justice—from immigrant rights to climate justice, voter registration, etc.—to seize this opportunity to explore and challenge what COVID-19 shows us about the hidden (and not-so-hidden) arrangements of our lives.
> —DS4SI, "Social Justice in a Time of Social Distancing," 2020

I am writing to you from the other end of a seven-day quarantine. It is August 29, 2021. We learned a week ago that our son's caregiver had tested positive for COVID-19 despite being vaccinated. Protocols were swiftly put into place. We tested ourselves, anxiously analyzed every sniffle, cough, and ache, and then tested ourselves again. This is the background and foreground to the interview that follows with Kenneth Bailey, sector organizing and strategy lead, and Lori Lobenstine, program design lead, who ask us to call attention to the forces that arrange our lives through their work at the Design Studio for Social Intervention (DS4SI).

I have known Bailey and Lobenstine for many years. We are thought partners and neighbors in the figurative and literal senses. I often appreciate their ability to call us to attend to both the ways in which our social and political lives are not only lived by us, in so far as we are able to exert agency over our lives, and how our lives are also being arranged, or designed, by visible and invisible forces. We are perhaps most familiar with this when it comes to the built environment. Every sidewalk, bus stop, ramp, or lack thereof, is part of a set of decisions made by appointed or elected authorities. Ideally these decisions are made through a democratic or community-centered process of some kind. Meetings are called, constituents polled. Often, however, these decisions are made for other reasons, for instance to appease business councils or for political reciprocity, and so on. This process migrates too. We, as residents of a given place, are being arranged not only by the built environment around us but also by policy, social norms, and perhaps most frequently by ideas. This is where Bailey, Lobenstine, and their work at DS4SI come in.

DS4SI is an artistic research and development outfit, as they write, "for the improvement of civil society and everyday life." For the better part of fifteen years, they have facilitated workshops, produced events, developed collaborative civic engagement projects, and published their findings in a series of essays and books. Most recently, they published the book *Ideas, Arrangements, Effects: Systems Design and Social Justice*, which we discuss below.[1] Written before the pandemic and published at the onset of the global lockdown in March 2020, *Ideas, Arrangements, Effects*

1
Kenneth Bailey and Lori Lobenstine, *Ideas, Arrangements, Effects: Systems Design and Social Justice* (Boston: DS4SI/ Minor Compositions, 2020).

makes the point that "ideas are embedded in social arrangements, which in turn produce effects." For example, "ideas like racism and sexism remain sturdy by embedding themselves in everything from physical and social infrastructure to everyday speech and thought habits," which produces kinds of arrangements—think gendered bathrooms or white-only drinking fountains—and in turn these arrangements produce effects. Effects can be additional ideas that reinforce these arrangements or the production of additional arrangements—think voting restrictions by gender or race.

Starting in March 2020 and continuing through 2021, Bailey and Lobenstine have published several smaller essays that complement and expand their thinking in *Ideas, Arrangements, Effects*. These include "Social Justice in a Time of Social Distancing," "What We Can Learn from White Terror in 2020," and "The Work after Our Rage," to name but a few.[2] Each of these essays calls us to bear witness to some detail within the compounding crises that we find ourselves in. Utilizing the *Ideas, Arrangements, Effects* framework, Bailey and Lobenstine urge us to allow our witnessing to attune us to the particularities of the crisis at hand, to sense the crisis as an effect of particular kinds of arrangements and ideas. It is through this cultivation of sense-making in relation to social and political crisis that Bailey and Lobenstine provide us with the means of intervening in and imagining more just and equitable arrangements.

Anthony Romero (AR): I thought we'd start with a bit of an introduction. What is the DS4SI?

Kenneth Bailey (KB): The studio has been around for about fifteen years. We bring artists, activists, and academics together to find new ways to attack social problems.

Lori Lobenstine (LL): We both come from a back-ground of community organizing and social justice. I

2
Kenneth Bailey and Lori Lobenstine, "Social Justice in a Time of Social Distancing," www.ds4si.org, 2020, https://www.ds4si.org/writings/socialjusticeinatimeofsocialdistance; Lori Lobenstine, "What We Can Learn from White Terror in 2020," www.ds4si.org, 2020, https://static1.squarespace.com/static/53c7166ee4b0e7db-2be69480/t/5ed-562f4a22a3463f-752be91/1591042804350/What+We+Can+Learn+-from+White+Ter-ror+in+2020.pdf; and Kenneth Bailey and Lori Lobenstine, "The Work after Our Rage," www.ds4si.org, 2020, https://static1.squarespace.com/static/53c7166ee4b0e7db-2be69480/t/5ed-5661218cb110bda3f57e9/1591043602858/TheWorkAfterOurRage_DS-4SI.pdf.

was doing youthwork, and Kenny was doing a lot of community organizing and development. We did a fellowship with Ceasar McDowell at the Center for Reflective Community Practice (CRCP) within MIT's Department of Urban Studies and Planning. It made us ask ourselves what tools designers had that we didn't, and how these tools might enable communities to imagine new solutions or come up with new approaches to addressing complex problems.

KB: We really want to think about the sensorial as well as the aesthetic dimensions of social worlds. We are interested in creating a space where the kinds of knowledge that circulate in contemporary art spaces meet up with the kinds of knowledge that circulate in activist and organizing spaces. We want to create a space that can function as a kind of epistemological meeting ground, where ways of understanding the world can come together to render new ways of imagining the world. That is one of the things we are still trying to crack: How do we create an opportunity for these ways of understanding to share space with each other?

LL: I would add that the idea of creating drafts and the idea of prototyping are important to our thinking. We sometimes miss those things in the worlds of social justice and nonprofits. We miss getting to test things and to learn what works and doesn't, versus having to pitch something to funders and act like you know what is going to work and then acting like it did work. With this wider lens of exploration and curiosity, we can see that maybe some things didn't go as expected, but it turned out beautifully in this other way, or some other thing unexpectedly happened altogether.

KB: Right. One of my fantasies is having a choreographer and an urban planner both look at people walking back and forth to the Red Sox's games at Fenway Park as a way of reading urban space—reading how they move through space wearing their

AN ECOLOGY OF ARRANGEMENTS

"costumes" of Red Sox apparel, etc. Why do these bodies get to take up so much of the spatial imaginary of Boston? And what does that mean for other bodies going other places? These kinds of collaborations or ways of making sense of the world aren't mainstream, and we don't have a lot of places to practice this kind of "sense-making."

We want the studio to be a space not just for sense-making but also for solution generation. Solution isn't even necessarily the right word. We are not necessarily trying to solve. It's more that we are trying to think of different ways to interfere with current arrangements.

AR: Let's turn to this past year, COVID-19, and the enduring social emergency, as you have described the proliferation of state-sanctioned violence. How have the last year and these compounding crises affected your work together?

KB: I think an emergent leap for us was coming to *Ideas, Arrangements, Effects* as a framework and then a book that helped us understand what we were doing. We were reading and having conversations—thinking about our own methodology—and it was just one of those things where the projects sort of organized themselves in this way that made sense.

LL: Kenny, you came back from New Zealand with the concept of how ideas are embedded in social arrangements that, in turn, produce effects. We realized that one of the things that was central to our work at that point was not only to help people sense arrangements, but also to intervene and imagine new arrangements. We combined that with our background in social justice and realized that together they helped us frame what we were doing.

AR: Can you expand a bit more about ideas and effects?

KB: The premise of the book *Ideas, Arrangements, Effects*, and this framework we're talking about, has as its operating thesis that ideas about the world, big and small, are embedded in social and cultural arrangements. For example, a set of chairs at a table is an arrangement that expresses a host of ideas. If the chairs are placed around the table, it suggests that a meal might be served. These kinds of arrangements can be hard and soft.

These things that we take for granted, these quotidian arrangements, are connected to each other. It's not like one arrangement does all of this work, but that we're in these social worlds created by overlapping arrangements. And these social worlds produce effects. So, if you're a person and you're organizing your way of understanding a problem around something like childhood obesity or state-sanctioned violence, your thinking is already organized in such a way that you are only seeing the effects. It is even evident in the names "childhood obesity" or "state-sanctioned violence." Naturalized operations, such as naming, are effects of the ordering of social worlds. If you are interested in actually doing something about these effects, then you have to organize your thinking to see the overarching, interconnected arrangements out of which these effects (childhood obesity, state-sanctioned violence) are produced.

Another example is the culture of believing that we need to be kept safe. That culture necessitates actual police forces and guns. If we go back further, we have the production of social space, urban space. You have to go back and look at all of these arrangements and start to work through them if you are trying to change their effects—cops killing Black people, childhood obesity, all that stuff.

LL: One of the things that folks who are fighting for social justice are good at is actually going from effects back to ideas. When you are thinking about big ideas, like understanding how and where racism plays out, or homophobia or xenophobia, it can be difficult to see how that idea is embedded in arrangements.

KB: It goes from large concepts to particular practices. For example, understanding the chairs and the table as a particular kind of arrangement allows you to do something about where the chairs go. You can throw the chair away, and you can come up with some other thing, but if you don't see that the chair is doing some work, or you don't see that the gun is doing some work, or if you don't see objects in relation to space, and time in relation to subjects, then you miss how ideas actually operate in the world. We feel like that's one of our gifts, to try and rethink how we create the social.

AR: Is there a direction to the *Ideas, Arrangements, Effects* framework, or is the idea that once you've become attuned to the framing then you can handle all three simultaneously?

KB: It's not a linear process. It's only linear when explaining it. It's almost like you can't explain simultaneously. We have to explain linearly, but the idea is for people to be able to see across all three rings with some level of complexity.

AR: Can we return to how your work and thinking have evolved over the last year? You explained to me previously that the book *Ideas, Arrangements, Effects* had already been written and was slated to come out before the pandemic. I find that to be quite prophetic since the book is about giving us the tools to sense how ideas arrange themselves around us and, in doing so, produce effects. Then comes a global pandemic that not only unveiled for us how our world had been arranged but also called us to rearrange ourselves in particular ways, through social distancing and quarantining, for example.

LL: One of the things that we have been pointing to since we published the essay "Social Emergency Procedures" is how hard it is for people to step out of their daily lives in order to really deal with a social emergency.[3] Suddenly we had a social emergency that forced us out of routine daily life and forced us to change arrangements, and yet it was met with a collective desire to "go back to normal." We found ourselves in a moment where we were saying, What if we didn't step back into normal life? What if we said we are going to stay out of everyday life until we figure out climate change, or we figure out police violence? We knew that asking for that pause and collective breath was asking a lot. We called for that pause earlier in "Social Emergency Procedures." We called for extending the time out of time and, with the pandemic, we called for it again.

KB: In a way, we propose pauses as a refusal to return to everyday life, a refusal to return to the quotidian that perpetuates these injustices. It's a different kind of protest. It's a refusal that's in solidarity with the protest we see happening right now in Amazonia, or what we see happening in Colombia. It is refusal as an act of protest that pulls away, not a protest of going out. Until we have some further reckoning along a particular line of inquiry, we're going on strike from everyday life. And we are going to try to make something that people can conceive of and actually practice as another technique of change. We see our participation in everyday life not as a given but as something about which we can say "Enough is enough" and withdraw from.

LL: I think it's also a strategy for solidarity, right? Folks most impacted by the problem have no choice. They've already been wrenched out of everyday life. Those of us who have the distance from the problem, either because of our class, race, or even location, we can continue everyday life. Instead of betraying our chance to say no, we need to say, "This is unacceptable." But where and how do you get to that step of being in solidarity?

KB: Even when stuff does affect us all, as with climate change, there is still some problem in our collective

AN ECOLOGY OF ARRANGEMENTS

consciousness that prevents us from saying or organizing our people to say "Enough is enough." We think a refusal of returning could potentially be a powerful way to at least stop long enough to start a new conversation. Pausing in and of itself is not the solution, but the stoppage creates an opportunity to breathe and to potentially start moving toward something new.

AR: I am curious how you all were feeling last summer, when it seemed, amid another summer of resurgent social movements, almost as though new social arrangements were emerging on top of each other?

KB: In terms of the movements, I think what we saw was an opportunity to help folks imagine and test out new worlds.

LL: One example of this is the opening provided by the uprisings to talk about abolition. The conversation brought in a much broader population than ever before, and we got to see people experimenting with some police-free zones, right? So, in that way, they were testing out new arrangements. We were asking ourselves, How do we map those things or help put those people in touch with each other? Or how to even think about what we learn, because this work is extremely difficult. There are the interventions into existing arrangements of policing, as well as the work of imagining and testing new arrangements of creating community safety without policing.

AR: How does this line of thinking become practice? How do you scale up the imagination?

KB: I think one of the things we're trying to figure out is how we might scale up the network of people with whom we co-imagine and move that out into the world. I think that's the next thing—trying to build a set of people who identify as being in this project of imagining alternative worlds.

LL: It feels like it's very hard to imagine new things. And so, the more ways that we can be a site for people who are eager to do that, the better. We need a broader range of examples, because some examples will speak to some people, and some to other people. Whatever you are trying to do, if there is an example that can get to you, you can have a "wow" moment. You can say, "I never thought of questioning the chair like that." How do we get to that thinking and imagining that might shift someone else's thinking in a way that prevents it from springing back so easily? How do you create rich examples for people, and how do you create partnerships with folks who can imagine and push those boundaries? I think this is how our creativity labs have functioned. They have either attracted folks who wanted to continue to think along these lines or have helped folks who haven't had the opportunity to think like that before.

AR: Is there some aspect of this that is about cultivating a kind of stereoscopic vision, which would allow one to keep multiple things in their field of vision at the same time?

KB: Lori and I were just talking about a project that would model that. The project would focus on an ecology of arrangements. You have people who are looking at the chair and at education, but they can't see how those arrangements are also connected, for example, to health centers, cities, and food. So, you always have to model what you're calling stereoscopic vision. We want to have the studio associated with that, as a way of approaching world making.

LL: When we think about arrangements, we tend to think about physical arrangements, right? But what would it mean for an educator to read that piece your collaborators wrote about spatial justice and the police siren, and then to investigate the sounds of the school?[4] The bell between classes, at least if you're in middle school or high school, does something. It tells you to do

4
Matt Joynt and Josh Rios, "Notes on the Siren and Social Space," in Kenneth Bailey, Lori Lobenstine, and Kiara Nagel, *Spatial Justice 2.0: A Frame for Reclaiming Our Rights to Be, Thrive, Express and Connect,* (Boston: DS4SI, 2020), p. 12–16, https://static1. squarespace.com/static/ 53c7166ee4b0e7db 2be69480/t/5e629 defadbcb60d977ec927 /1583521265858/ spatial_ justice_zine_digital.pdf

something, and you have a limited time to do it. So, if I'm thinking with artists, like your collaborators, who are thinking about the symbolic power of sound, we can extend that thinking to a set of educators who are thinking about the school day.

KB: And concretely put that together with the principal, and be like, "You guys are responsible for thinking about the school, starting with the chair and the bell."

AR: That's part of what I was thinking about when I mentioned stereoscopic vision. How do we cultivate the capacity to see not only each individual arrangement, but also each individual arrangement in relation to every other? And how many things constitute an arrangement in the first place?

KB: Exactly, it's always more than one.

AR: There are two things that are continuing to circle around in my head. One is the pause—the breath—that you talked about and that you've written about. And the other is the refusal to return or to participate—to continue to participate. A refusal, even, to be complicit in certain arrangements. In some ways, it seems to be in contrast to the kinds of refusals we saw during the riot at the Capitol, or in regard to police reform, or other shifts in culture, policy, or thinking that might be met with a type of "white refusal," to give it a name. This is perhaps a long way of asking, Are there different kinds of refusals? Different scales to these kinds of pauses or interruptions? Do you think they need to be paired with certain shifts in consciousness in order to ensure that you're not complicit in forming or reproducing uneven arrangements?

LL: It is true that even in forming new arrangements, we can bring our whole clumsy, racist, classist what-have-you to the process. I have thought about that. I mean, where are we going to get with a new arrangement with our old selves? You know, we'll be back to our smallness and ugliness, perpetuating ideas about those who have and have not. You ask a really hard question.

KB: It's partly about shaping those conversations, because some of us will be pausing while others will be very busy creating the conditions for us to convene, think, and work together. Some of us will be busy holding the space. We have to see it along the lines of ontological design—becoming new subjects. We have to see it as a kind of test case for remaking subjects that could be. In these pauses—even if they're not direct—it's not only an ontological test. We are asking you to step into a new way of being a subject.

LL: One of the ways that we have thought about that—which might be our optimistic or hopeful way of approaching it—is to make space for collective sense-making as part of the pause, and to try to do that not just at the large scale of protest and refusal but also at the small scale of creating space for those conversations. So, it's not just "We're all going to pause, and we're all going to go to the Capitol to make our point," but "What conversations are we having with our families, at our places of worship, or with our neighbors?" Not just some, but all the neighbors, the ones who do and don't talk to us. What are we trying to change, and how might we change because we're in conversation?

One of the things that we have had success with is when we create a new arrangement and people get to try new things; it helps us actually be in a different conversation. A lot of time, as activists, our tendency is to get straight to the point, like, "No police!" "Fuck the police!," etc. And that's really important, and I believe in that wholeheartedly, but that's not going to get me anywhere in terms of a conversation with someone whose dad is a police officer.

     AN ECOLOGY OF ARRANGEMENTS

KB: Or someone who doesn't want the police but also doesn't want to be held up at gunpoint.

LL: Yes, thank you for that. Sometimes the conversation has to be about something else entirely, about spareribs, or our elders losing their memories, or springtime. We have to create space where we come together to get to know each other and provide resources to each other, not because we're having a political conversation, agreeing or disagreeing, but because we're having a conversation with each other. That's an aspiration for public life, right? Being humans to each other first and then, from there, what can we imagine?

KB: And, while that's happening, we're making preparations to get from a neighborhood that's organized around police to a neighborhood that's been reorganized in such a way that, when the power vacuum of police has been pulled out, it doesn't fall apart.

This interview took place on July 13, 2021.

THEN X ENTERS

Damon Locks

The following body of work emerged while I was teaching through correspondence at Stateville Correctional Center, a maximum-security state prison in Crest Hill, Illinois, through the Prison and Neighborhood Arts/Education Project (PNAP), a visual arts and education project that connects teaching artists and scholars with incarcerated students at Stateville. The course I taught was called 51st (Free) State Comics, and my own response to it was a collection of eighteen piece that were presented together in the exhibition *Then X Enters* at Goldfinch Gallery in Chicago in the spring of 2020.

51st (Free) State Comics

This class explores the graphic novel/comic. Our goal is to create a collection/anthology of comic-book pages based around the ideas generated and inspired by Sarah Ross's Anthem class and Martine Whitehead's movement score class. We will generate work around the concept of the 51st state: resilience, justice, injustice, surveillance, identity, belonging, brilliance, imagination, freedom, transcendence. I am also aware that the environment you are living in is even more precarious than ever, and I think this class is tailor-made to support you however you need. We are working toward a truly just world. We are here to explore all aspects of that.

Whether you need to address this world as we find it right at this moment or you need to imagine a radically new one, these assignments can be interpreted to suit your needs.

1. Make a four-panel comic strip of drawings about having a conversation with yourself on the subject of liberation. The character(s) are all you. There could be just one figure or there could be ten, but there must be a character.

2. Imagine a place that doesn't exist anymore. Maybe it disappeared, maybe it was destroyed, maybe over time it withered away, maybe it was taken over. This place can be a fantastical place: another world, underground, in the sky, etc. This place can be a literal space: a bookstore, community center, a place you once lived, etc. This place can be an idea: harmony, justice, unity, etc. As far as *how you tell the story*, you can approach this any way that suits you: someone could be interviewing you or someone else about this place, you/someone could be remembering it on the eve of its disappearance, or it could be a report on the TV or radio about the place.

3. This will be part one of two parts. The theme will be change and transformation. We are thinking with changing minds and transforming spaces/neighborhoods/worlds/institutions/etc.

Here are things to think about while developing part one of the story:

1. What is the setting? Establish where the story takes place.

2. What is the issue? Establish the problems faced.

3. What forces a change? What makes the story change, requiring things to transform?

4. What is the beginning of transformation? How can you leave the reader wanting more?

Since this is part one of two parts, we need to think about *suspense*. The end of this should come *right before* or *right at* the moment of change. The reader will have to wait until the next issue to find out what happens!

Then X Enters

The exhibition *Then X Enters* focused on the *X* as it walks into our lives. We live with it. We work around it. We fear it. We seek to know it. This system of drawing and collage deals in the unknown. The image builds itself one step at a time. The stance and position must find their footing with shifting plates below them. The effect is destabilizing yet full of possibility. In the making, one cannot race ahead to see how things turn out. You, the viewer, patiently go through the transformations in time to see what new form has revealed itself as *X* prepares to announce its intentions.

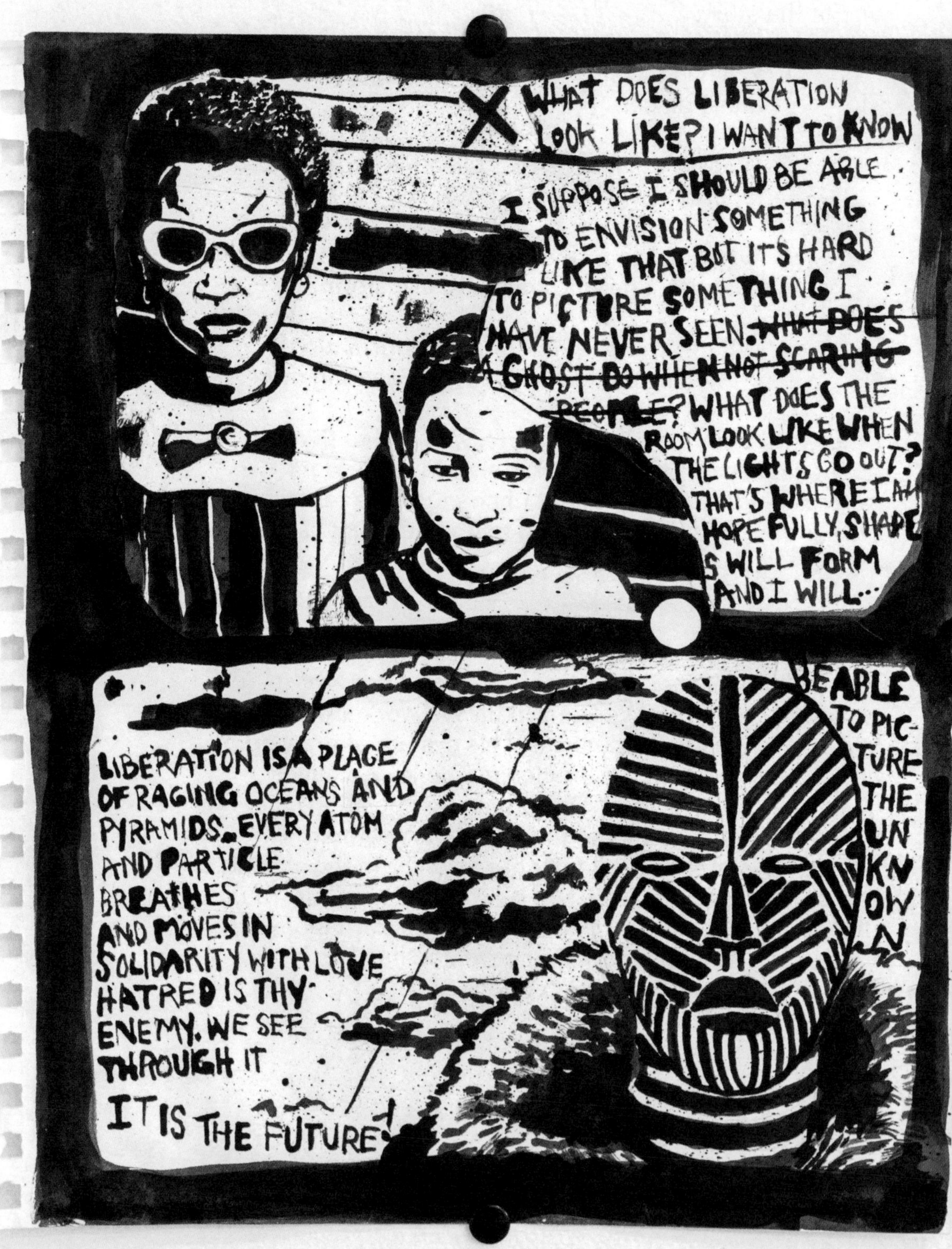
X WHAT DOES LIBERATION LOOK LIKE? I WANT TO KNOW
I SUPPOSE I SHOULD BE ABLE TO ENVISION SOMETHING LIKE THAT BUT IT'S HARD TO PICTURE SOMETHING I HAVE NEVER SEEN. WHAT DOES A GHOST DO WHEN NOT SCARING PEOPLE? WHAT DOES THE ROOM LOOK LIKE WHEN THE LIGHTS GO OUT? THAT'S WHERE I AM HOPEFULLY, SHADES WILL FORM AND I WILL...
BE ABLE TO PICTURE THE UNKNOWN
LIBERATION IS A PLACE OF RAGING OCEANS AND PYRAMIDS. EVERY ATOM AND PARTICLE BREATHES AND MOVES IN SOLIDARITY WITH LOVE HATRED IS THY ENEMY. WE SEE THROUGH IT
IT IS THE FUTURE!

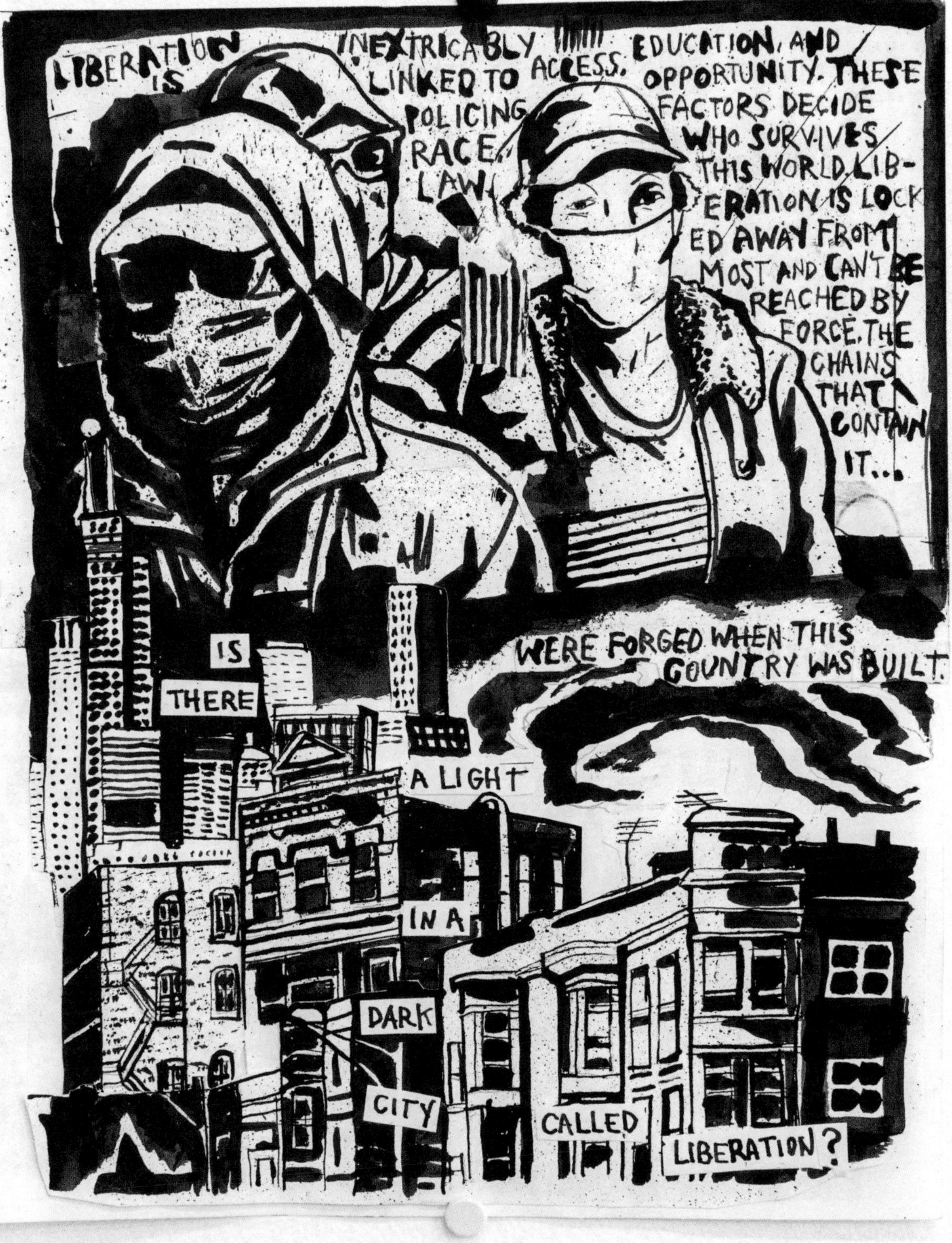

LIBERATION IS INEXTRICABLY LINKED TO ACCESS, EDUCATION, AND OPPORTUNITY. THESE FACTORS DECIDE WHO SURVIVES THIS WORLD. LIBERATION IS LOCKED AWAY FROM MOST AND CAN'T BE REACHED BY FORCE. THE CHAINS THAT CONTAIN IT...

POLICING
RACE.
LAW.

WERE FORGED WHEN THIS COUNTRY WAS BUILT.

IS THERE A LIGHT IN A DARK CITY CALLED LIBERATION?

WE

FOUND THE CONDITIONS WERE UNTENABLE, LIVES WERE BROKEN BY REPEATED THUNDER CLAPS, & LIGHTNING WITH NO RAIN, A BLINDING LIGHT ENVELOPED CHOKING OUT GROWTH WHERE SEEDLINGS POKED THROUGH. SIRENS BLARED AT THE HIGHEST VOLUMES REACHING THE FURTHEST CORNERS OF THE UNIVERSE. WE NEED ROCKET SHIPS.

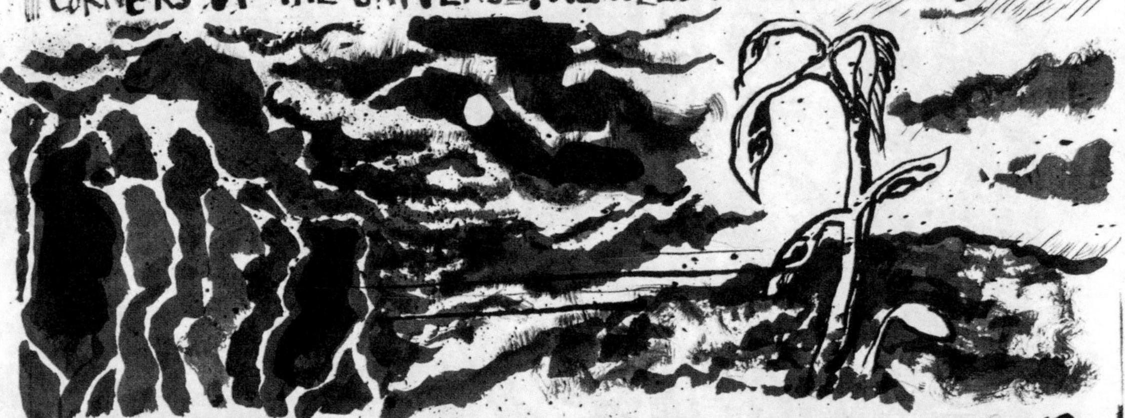

MUST

BREATHING STOP AT THE EDGE OF THE SKY? NO! WE CAN RECONFIGURE. THE MIND COLLAPSES INTO SPACE, THE BODY WRAPS AROUND IT. THERE IS FERTILE SOIL ON THE EDGE OF UNKNOWING. ABUNDANT ARE THE FRUITS THAT SWEETEN THE TONGUE

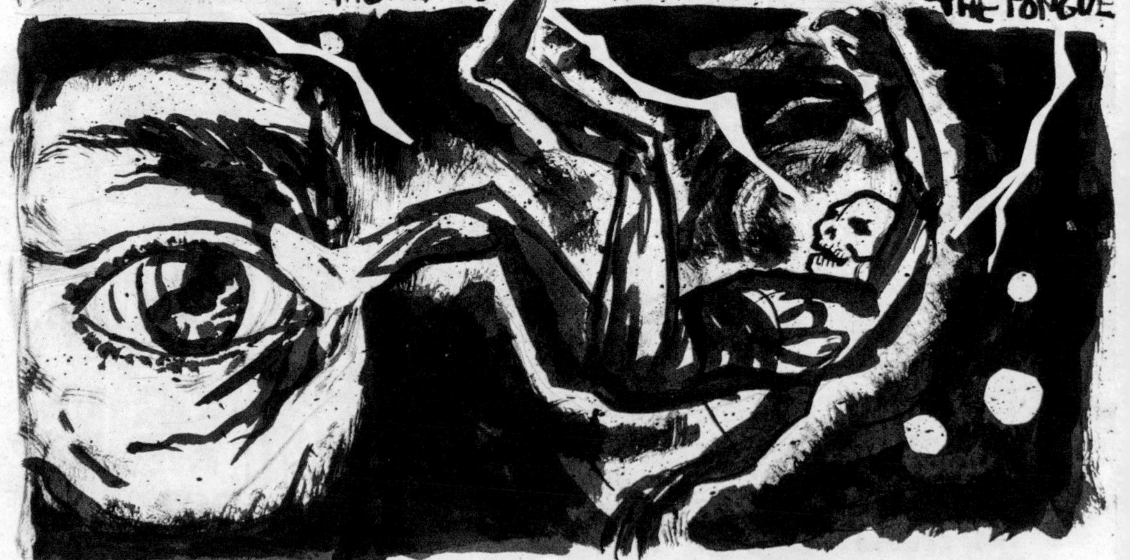

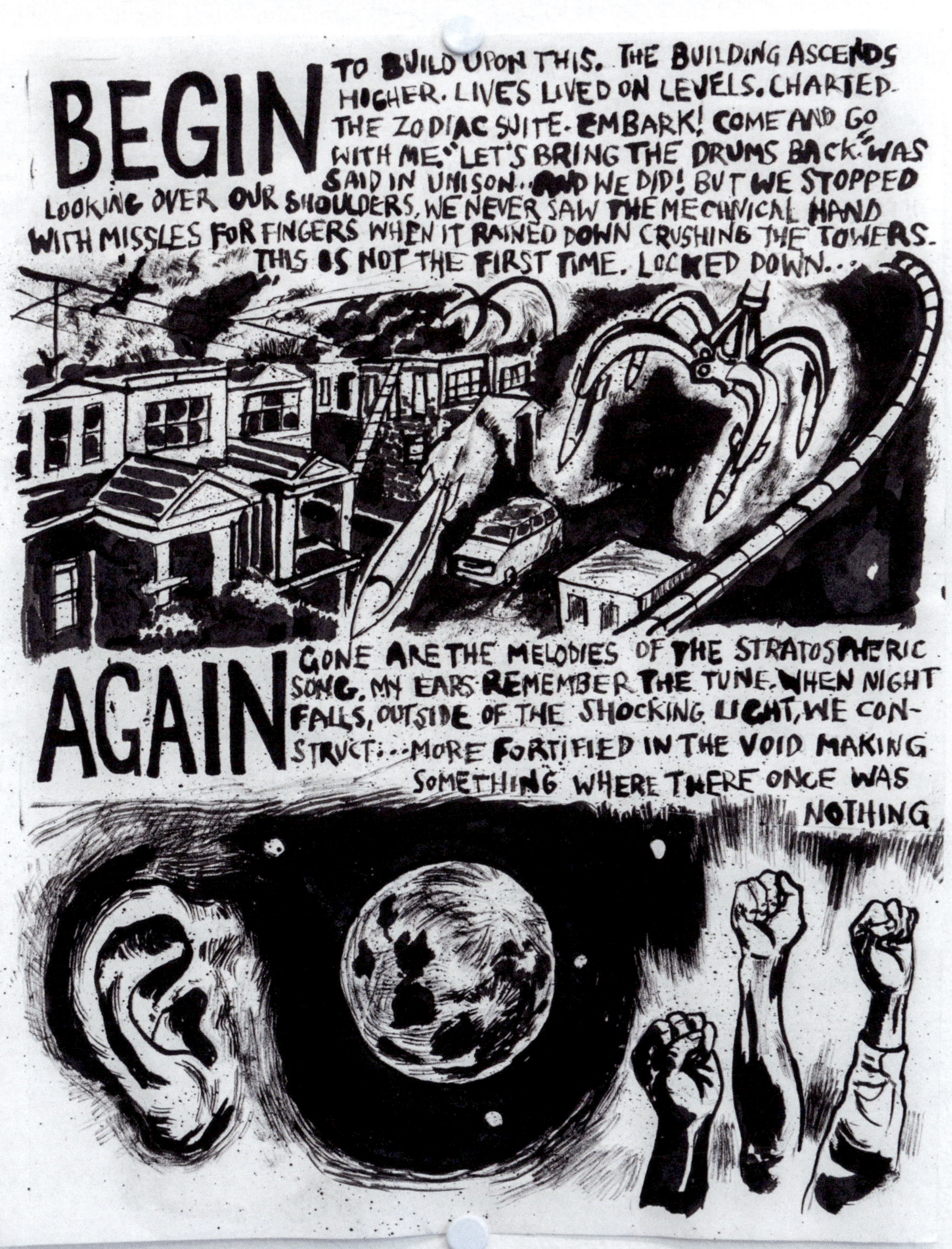

BEGIN TO BUILD UPON THIS. THE BUILDING ASCENDS HIGHER. LIVES LIVED ON LEVELS. CHARTED. THE ZODIAC SUITE. EMBARK! COME AND GO WITH ME. "LET'S BRING THE DRUMS BACK" WAS SAID IN UNISON... AND WE DID! BUT WE STOPPED LOOKING OVER OUR SHOULDERS, WE NEVER SAW THE MECHNICAL HAND WITH MISSLES FOR FINGERS WHEN IT RAINED DOWN CRUSHING THE TOWERS. THIS IS NOT THE FIRST TIME. LOCKED DOWN...

AGAIN GONE ARE THE MELODIES OF THE STRATOSPHERIC SONG, MY EARS REMEMBER THE TUNE. WHEN NIGHT FALLS, OUTSIDE OF THE SHOCKING LIGHT, WE CONSTRUCT... MORE FORTIFIED IN THE VOID MAKING SOMETHING WHERE THERE ONCE WAS NOTHING

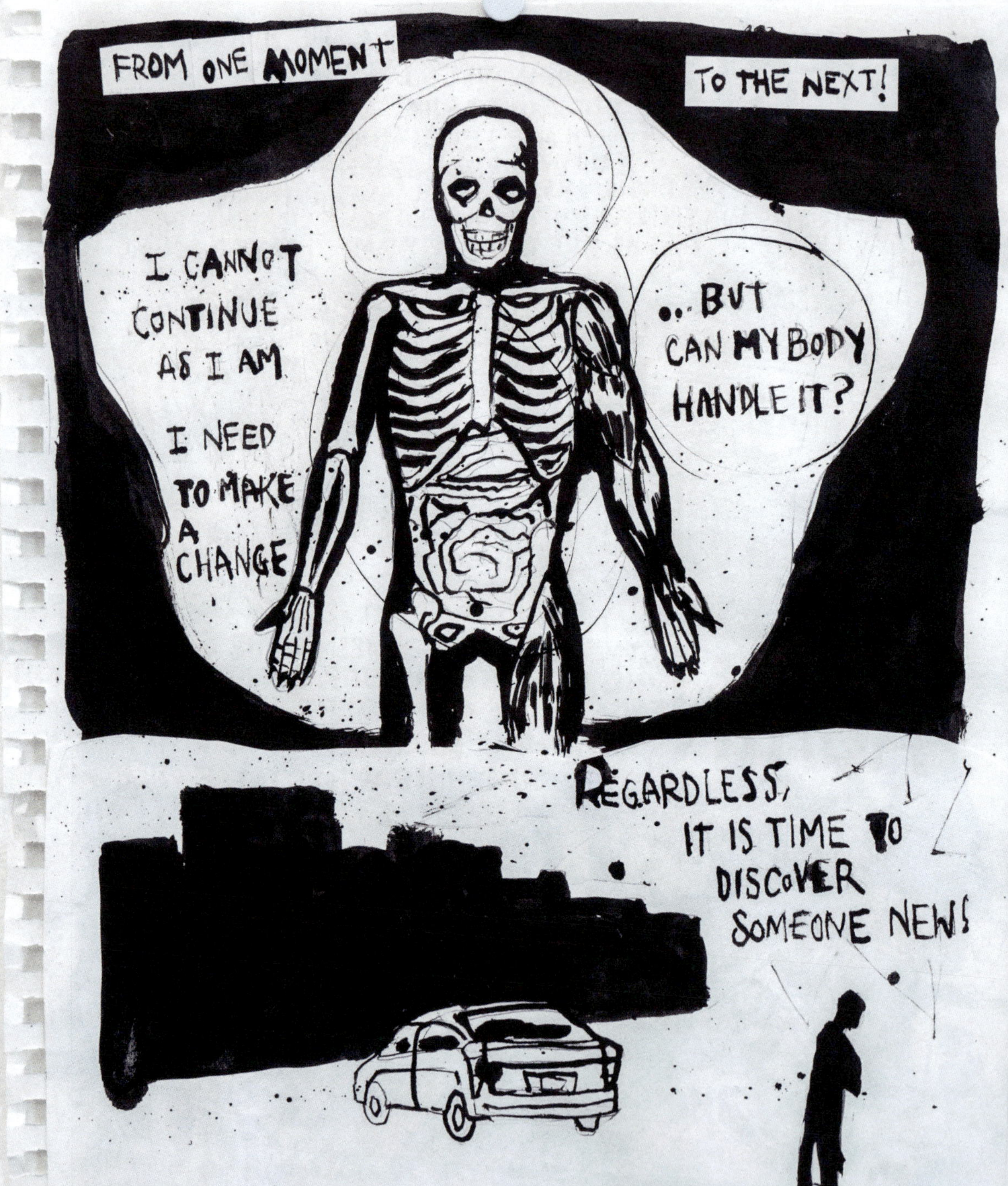

FROM ONE MOMENT
TO THE NEXT!
I CANNOT CONTINUE AS I AM
I NEED TO MAKE A CHANGE
..BUT CAN MY BODY HANDLE IT?
REGARDLESS, IT IS TIME TO DISCOVER SOMEONE NEW!

SILENCE WON'T SAVE YOU:
An Interview with Kelli Morgan

Daniel Tucker

I met Kelli Morgan at an art opening in September 2016, a few months after she began her position as the Winston & Carolyn Lowe Curatorial Fellow for Diversity in the Fine Arts at the Pennsylvania Academy of Fine Arts (PAFA). Given that PAFA is a notoriously sleepy institution, it was thrilling to meet someone there who had a passion for early American art and design and, as a scholar with an African American studies degree, could contextualize them both art historically and in terms of their relationship to the history of race in the United States. Morgan became a friend and colleague, sharing her insights with the classes I brought to her exhibits and collaborating on public programs about cultural equity and museums in Philadelphia.[1] Morgan's generosity of engagement, sharp analysis, and quick wit made her a pleasure to be around and a force in the classroom and the gallery alike.

   In 2018 Morgan left Philadelphia when she was tapped by the Indianapolis Museum of Art (IMA) at

[1] "Blake Bradford, Maori Holmes, Kelli Morgan, & Damon Reeves," December 7, 2016, Conversations@ Moore lecture series, "Who Is We? Intersecting Engagement and Equity Efforts at Philadelphia's Art Institutions," Philadelphia, PA, https://conversationsarchive.wordpress.com /2016/12/07/blake-bradford-maori-holmes-kelli-morgan-damon-reeves/. As a prompt, this series used the essay "Making Sense of Cultural Equity," Createquity, August 2016, http://createquity.com/2016/08/making-sense-of-cultural-equity/.

Newfields to be the associate curator of American art. Her intentions upon arrival were unambiguous; a 2019 article featured a tour of her gallery redesign, which quoted her wall text: "What happens when American art is interpreted through its multiple social and political contexts instead of its aesthetic and art historical merit?"[2]

We fell out of touch and then, in the summer of 2020, Morgan publicly resigned from the IMA. The resignation drew national media attention and significant support for Morgan, who sent her resignation letter to board members, local arts leaders, and the *Indianapolis Star* newspaper.[3] Ultimately, this solitary act required that Morgan assume all of the risk involved in calling out a toxic and racist workplace, and it was not until February 2021 that she was vindicated.

On February 12, 2021, an IMA job posting for a museum director was published on both the museum's website and on the m/Oppenheim Executive Search website (it has since been removed from both), which included a line about the museum's need to maintain a "core, white art audience" while it expanded to include new diverse audiences. On February 16, current IMA employees called for the resignation of the museum's president, Charles L. Venable,[4] and articles followed in the *New York Times* and *Hyperallergic*, among others.[5] By February 17, Venable had submitted his resignation. Throughout this process, Morgan was actively posting on her social media accounts, giving interviews to the press, and consulting with her former coworkers.

Our conversation the following week covered this event as it was happening, as well as the larger wave of grassroots demands for institutional responses to racial injustice and pandemic-induced museum worker precarity. We discussed these calls for change within the context of Morgan's familial history and formative art experiences, her scholarly work on Black feminist visuality, and her years of curatorial experience in museums, including the Birmingham Museum of Art and PAFA.

2
"Dr. Kelli Morgan Brings Diversity to Newfields," NUVO, July 4, 2019, https://nuvo.newsnirvana. com/arts/dr-kelli-morgan-brings-diversity-to-newfields/article_ c5f88892-9dd4-11e9-b17b-53b058625072.html.

3
Domenica Bongiovanni, "Curator Calls Newfields Culture Toxic, Discriminatory in Resignation Letter," *Indianapolis Star*, July 18, 2020, https://www. indystar.com/story/ entertainment/arts/2020 /07/18/newfields-curator-says-discriminatory-workplace-toxic/5459574002/.

4
"An Open Letter from a Group of Concerned Newfields Staff," Google Docs, February 16, 2021, https://drive.google.com/ file/d/1FjZU-bMq4lUz-JcpLIVgJ83SeBa7Yq5h1/ view.

5
Valentina Di Liscia, "1,500+ Call for Museum President's Removal after Job Posting Cites 'Core, White Art Audience,'" Hyperallergic, February 16, 2021, https:// hyperallergic.com/622418/ indianapolis-call-for-museum-presidents-removal-job-posting-white-art-audience/.

Daniel Tucker (DT): I'd like to draw some attention to how the intergenerational relationships in your life formed the foundation of your thinking about Black material culture.

Kelli Morgan (KM): Oh, they totally did. My interest in Black material culture comes directly from playing with my grandfather. I used to do this thing as a six-year-old, seven-year-old kid. We were not a huge church family, so on Sundays, if it was raining or if my friends were gone at church, I would go into the attic and I would pull out, I mean, just all kinds of stuff. I would sit there and make up stories about a particular *Life Magazine* or a Coke bottle from the 1920s, which were there because my grandfather was born in 1912. These old things fascinated me.

Now, as an adult, I look back and remember that my grandfather would come up to the attic and give me the whole rundown about what was happening in the country, why these objects were in the attic, what the family story was as to whose objects they were. I remember that, as I got older, he began to say, "Come here, Kelli!" and we would sit down and flip through *National Geographic* or the *Smithsonian Magazine*, which he got because he shined shoes for a living. He worked in the plants, too, but lost his index finger in a stamping accident, so he started to shine shoes at the racetrack. We would go through these magazines and discuss the artwork. He didn't have the magazines every time he came home from work, so the nights when he did were always such a treat.

I remember viewing one that was about the decorative arts—plates, tea services, and those kinds of things. I vividly remember him walking me through it, saying, "Does this remind you of anything?" And I was kinda like, "No, but it's pretty." Then he would walk me through how my grandmother entertained when everybody came over for the holidays, and I was like, "Oh, yeah! It looks like grandma's stuff, but hers isn't as ornate." My grandmother's tea services, china, and flatware were very modern, and the objects in the magazine were colonial American decorative art. But it made sense to me. I was able to draw a connection—my Grams was using her objects for the same things the magazine discussed. And my grandfather continued to draw these connections for me with painting and other art objects, too.

So, my recognition of objects and museums—once I got into my twenties and thirties—was always through people I knew who utilized similar objects. Something that I've said about my relationship to art is that it was not developed through the museum—it literally grew out of my grandmother's dining room. European art for me wasn't the Met; it was my mother's mantle. That was my access. It took me thirty years to put that together, but it's always been there. This attention to people centers my curatorial practice, and my interest in art and material culture grows out of and has a lot to do with my relationship to my family.

DT: Thanks for narrating that. It's really incredible to be able to locate those kinds of origins. Continuing with that, I was thinking about how your PhD dissertation is focused on the idea of Black feminist visuality and the work of "self-making" and how that's visualized. What kind of curatorial practice comes from that lens? To some extent, I'm asking what your curatorial approach is, but I'm also drawing on what you said about relationships and how that figures into the approach.

KM: I think my curatorial approach is actually my own expression of Black feminist visuality. I define it as the way that Black women assert their autonomy and subjectivity—a spirit of self-making, through how they utilize representational female bodies. So these practices are either photographs of themselves or the ways that they're literally making bodies, right—whether they're carving wood or stone—because in crafting the theory, I looked primarily at sculptors. Even though I am not necessarily working with Black women artists or

     SILENCE WON'T SAVE YOU

Black women's narratives in all of my curatorial projects, my curatorial approach is still a Black woman's narrative because that is my view of the world.

I like to say that I work from the outside into the object. For me, it is about how people activate objects with their own narratives, be it directly or indirectly. That kind of assertion of autonomy and subjectivity goes beyond me as the curator. I am trying to use an object, whatever it is—painting, installation, sculpture, decorative art—to communicate several different subjectivities and several different autonomies with respect to citizenship, humanity, and art history—particularly for people of color, because we aren't always allowed that in the museum space. I assert my own Black feminist visuality to illuminate everybody's relationships to and under-standings of particular objects. I feel like you don't necessarily have to have an art history training from Yale to appreciate a Tiffany window. I'm really trying to level the playing field in a way, to eradicate classism and elitism.

DT: Continuing with that, I am wondering about your lens as a scholar coming from African American studies into the museum. Why does that lens and why do those skills—analytical, research, critical race theory (CRT)—become useful in a museum? I am curious about that training and what it facilitates in this moment in terms of skills . . . and in contrasting these skills with the kinds of skills people have often brought into museums as a result of other kinds of disciplinary training.

KM: The most concrete example that I can use to illustrate that is that, as a Black studies scholar, I was trained to study the functionality of whiteness through a Black cultural lens. Therefore, I study systemic racism, white privilege, and white supremacy in the same way that art historians study whatever area of art history they specialize in.

I also have a tremendous command of Black culture. Some of my Black studies colleagues explain how you may meet people of color who *feel* Blackness, because, of course, they experience it in a very literal way. But then there are people like us, who are both Black and scholars of Blackness, so we actually *know* Blackness in a very specific way—meaning, we know it as an academic, political, cultural, and intellectual framework. We know its tenets, its rules, its functionality. We know how Black cultural practices function, both historically and currently. We know what they were created for, how Black people used them, and why. An illustration of this is explaining how hip-hop was and continues to be a response to capitalism and gentrification, whereas, if you ask a lay Black person, hip-hop is a piece of them. It is a personal expression. And this type of functionality applies to any group's cultural practices, not just Black folks'.

For instance, it's not like enslaved Africans woke up every day planning to go resist white supremacy. They got up every day and did what they did. Now, many of those activities were acts of resistance, both passive and direct. I think that's the difference when you are a scholar—you know Black culture in a very deep way while also knowing how it responds to the reality of race, racism, and whiteness.

To offer a personal example, I've come to understand that no museum that I've worked for to date hired me because of my actual specialty in CRT and anti-racism. They hired me because of what I look like. They hired me because I was Black, checking the diversity box. I stepped into PAFA and the IMA at Newfields as a scholar-curator who keenly understands the white supremacist, capitalist, patriarchal systems under which the museum staff, leadership, and objects operate and which they uphold. And now that the third institution I've worked for has responded in a very negative, reactionary way to the work that I do to disrupt and eradicate those systems, I understand the functionality and mechanisms of those systems as normal and foundational to museum culture. So much so that their dismantling would undo the entire institution, which is something that art museums are fighting hard to prevent from happening—although I think they're losing that fight.

My work is inherently disruptive. As a Black studies scholar, I'm trained to see the absences. I'm trained to read the silences. So I can glean a whole lot more from what a label leaves out, or from what is missing from an archive, than from what is actually there. More specifically to my resignation from Newfields, I was able to apply this to the institution's overall racist culture. Meaning, I was able to recognize the ways in which the institution's racism undermined me and my colleagues' work. For instance, I remember the moment when the marketing department decided that it would not market the Samuel Levi Jones exhibition to Black communities despite the fact that it was the institution's first solo show of a Black Indiana artist, curated by the museum's first Black curator and first Asian curator of performance. Instead of documenting this decision in the exhibition's communications strategy, which was developed for all of the institution's exhibitions and programs, it was something that was communicated verbally—mind you, only to me.

Or the time I was told that curators weren't allowed to give tours in their own galleries. This was the institution's initial reaction to how frequently I toured BIPOC school groups. Of course, I knew that was foolish, and I continued to tour Black and Latinx kids from all around the city. Because I wouldn't stop, the institution then trained me on its process for booking docent and school group tours, which included a "new" category for curator-led tours. They were very careful in their methods of discrimination in that these directives were never written down; they were always communicated verbally.

I also utilized my expertise to combat the institution's egregious tone-deafness and racism when I responded to racist remarks made by one of the institution's most beloved white donors during a September 2019 art committee meeting. While discussing the acquisition of Roberto Lugo's *The Expulsion of*

Colin Kaepernick and John Brown, this particular donor made a racist remark about Kaepernick's decision to kneel on the sideline during the national anthem. When I explained the historical contexts of African American protest against white supremacy and how costly that protest is for any American and how critical this specific racial history is to the design of Lugo's vase—the work depicts Kaepernick on one side and abolitionist John Brown on the other—it was determined by senior leadership that I had acted unprofessionally. Meaning that I was not supposed to "speak" to a high-level donor with any authority.

The leadership attempted to shame me in subsequent meetings for speaking up about *The Expulsion of Colin Kaepernick and John Brown*, suggesting that I didn't have the right to say anything in these meetings because the artwork was not technically "my" acquisition. Meaning, it was not an artwork that I was presenting for acquisition to the American collection. This demonstrated the leadership's utter lack of understanding of Black cultural objects within their cultural contexts, as well as its complete ignorance of my expertise. Ultimately, all these things, coupled with the psychological and emotional trauma from the first meeting and the ways in which the leadership continued to attack me afterward, led to my resignation and my decision to speak publicly about how abusive art museum leaders often are. I have never in my life experienced such blatant racism anywhere, and I pray that I never will again.

DT: I am struck by how, in this moment, the rise in the visibility of Black art is concurrent with the internal struggles that are happening within arts institutions among the people who are employed there. Reflecting back on what you were saying about what is seen, I am wondering what your take is on what is seen or unseen in the space of the museum?

KM: The artist Carl Pope explains this in such an eloquent way; this is something he and I talk about

SILENCE WON'T SAVE YOU

regularly. Carl is a printmaker and photographer who was very popular in the '80s and '90s. Making his acquaintance when I arrived in Indianapolis was one of my best decisions! He describes it like this: it is feigned attention to Black subjectivity for the purpose of economic gain for a particular set of individuals at the expense of actual Black subjectivity.

This makes sense in the neoliberal, capitalist era that we're living in, where the idea is that if we advance a very select group or, in certain cases, person, to a high economic position in the field, then discrimination and racism will stop. I've experienced this sentiment among senior museum professionals, both Black and white, where they're like, "The racism or discrimination that Dr. Kelli Morgan is complaining about isn't really a problem because Nick Cave is a whole phenomenon. Or because Mark Bradford and Simone Leigh represented the US in the Biennale. Or because Thelma Golden and Lonnie Bunch are so well respected and highly positioned in museums."

And yes, they all are. But everyday BIPOC museum professionals are experiencing life-altering discrimination within art museums and so many more Black artists are being marginalized or completely overlooked by the art market than are being uplifted. I have always been adamant in stating that *both* realities are true. Not to take anything away from how great those artists and directors are and not to say that they don't totally deserve the attention they receive, but on any given day, let them be in the wrong place at the wrong time as a Black person . . . let a cop or, hell, even just a regular, everyday white person feel "afraid." In such circumstances, nobody will care that they're amazing Black contemporary artists or museum directors.

So if we know that's possible, in terms of the larger society, how are we not applying that knowledge to addressing what is actually happening to Black museum professionals every day, and also to emerging and mid-career Black contemporary artists every day, and that it's primarily perpetuated by the field's most well-known museum directors, chief curators, and gallery owners? That may not bother folks in the field who are the one-percenters or a part of the Black elite, because attaining that level of success has been their struggle and something they've worked hard for, but that doesn't mean that discrimination suddenly stopped because a select group of BIPOC artists and museum professionals reached a high level of success in the field. Honestly, it's gotten worse *because* of their visibility, primarily because the visibility of Black artists and the rising number of Black curators and directors makes it a lot easier for the field to say, "Well, it's not as bad as it used to be." Which is a response that is often used to try to silence people like me—those of us who are fighting blatant and deliberate acts of racism within art institutions every day.

You also have to consider other museum professionals and artists who are dedicated to anti-racist work and who are being abused, ignored, and erased. The same thing is happening to Native American artists and curators; and LGBTQI artists and museum professionals, conservators, preparators, and registrars the field over. And it hasn't even changed in terms of white women; though, as bad as gender discrimination is, sometimes white women are the worst perpetrators of white, racist patriarchy in the field.

It's 2021, so the field is like thirty to thirty-five years out from consistent exhibitions of women artists and artists of color. There have been thousands of acquisitions . . . and the racist, sexist, classist culture of art museums still hasn't changed. At what point are we going to admit that exhibitions are not enough? Hiring BIPOC curators isn't enough. Deaccessioning to acquire artworks by BIPOC artists isn't enough. Because ultimately, representation isn't enough. Diversity is *not enough* because getting us through the door, or "at the table" so to speak, is actually *not* the problem. The problem is a funding model that depends almost exclusively on the wealth of very problematic and often-

    SILENCE WON'T SAVE YOU

times racist individuals. And if me, Chaédria LaBouvier, Andrea Montiel de Shuman, Porchia Moore, LaTanya Autry, and Mike Murawski are the only ones out here brave enough to say it publicly and to attach ourselves firmly to that truth, then that's just what it has to be.

DT: We're having this conversation in a particular time where some of that bravery is manifesting. It has been manifesting for a while, but it is now manifesting in some organizational changes. Six months after your public resignation because of white supremacist workplace culture, there has been a storm of organizing within the last few weeks in response to the IMA's February 12, 2020, job posting, in which they advertised the museum's intent to maintain their "core, white art audience."

I'm wondering about your reflections on how this relates to what you were saying about the arc of institutional representation. I want to hear your thoughts on what is lost under bad leadership but also on what it takes to create actual institutional change. What do you think about how leadership obscures people's work internally and how it works when there is a leadership transition?

KM: I always say that I may not always be able to fix it or change it, but I will always say something. This came from my experience at PAFA. I didn't speak out publicly in Philly and, after I left, that administration systematically undermined the rest of my colleagues. Sometimes I've felt like had I said something, that wouldn't have happened. Sometimes I think, "God. I should have fought harder."

The fact is that these administrations know exactly what they're doing. Their point of view is "What can you do about it? Who is going to believe you?" Because the culture of silence and fear is just that significant. They don't think we'll ever say anything publicly because the field socializes us not to. I can remember certain folks in my trajectory who were like, "You have to stop doing that, Kelli. You're never going to get a job. Oh my god Kelli . . . You don't want to be labeled the angry Black woman. You just can't do that." And I said, "Maybe you feel that way, but I don't." And by the time I got to the IMA, I was sick of it. I wasn't gonna deal with the bad behavior any longer, and I think it took the IMA leadership by surprise that I wouldn't stop fighting against their problematic behavior—I would never just sit there and be the token Black girl they wanted me to be. There were so many times where the lash-out or retaliation was painful and very harmful. But I took up this "Fuck you, I'm from Detroit" mentality. Meaning, I've never been afraid to fight. I may not always win, but I'm definitely gonna land some punches.

I witnessed a museum leadership—and a museum director in particular—that was used to never being called on its racist behavior. They were so used to doing whatever they wanted, basically just steamrolling people, ruling with an iron fist of fear. That fear was really serious. There were *so many* brilliant, talented people who left IMA because they just couldn't be there any more under such abusive leadership. It was watching that happen, watching my colleagues go from super optimistic to "I'm just gonna put my head down and do my job because I don't want to be bothered with it anymore" that was devastating for me. Those colleagues who resigned just before me, who lost their entire lives, basically, because they couldn't work in the city anymore, had to pick up and move across the damn country, losing their entire social circle . . . leaving their extended families, etc. It was devastating to watch! These institutions play chess with our lives.

I was like, "Oh no, not anymore if I can do something about it." And again, I felt like "He may get away with it and nobody may believe me, but I gotta say something." As much as we tried to advocate for ourselves and to petition the board . . . I mean, people have been doing it for years, going to particular board members and saying things. I spoke to three different board members upon my exit, and only one was brave enough to speak up in the board meeting that took place after I exited. But no matter how much we said to board members, nothing ever changed. And after a while, the staff became discouraged.

There were a few Black museum professionals who were fighting this fight in the '80s, who were fighting this fight in the '70s; they didn't win their fights either, or get widespread support. One older Black female curator—she was so sweet—called me in July, just before my resignation. We had never met before, so I was unfamiliar with her work, but she asked, "How do you still have a job!? What's the young lady's name in Cleveland?" I said, "LaTanya Autry," and she said, "Yes, I am just so in awe of you girls, but how are y'all still working!?" And I said, "By the skin of our teeth! LOL!!" Then she said, "Keep doing what you are doing but be careful because there's a consequence that comes with what you're doing." It was so sweet to hear from her at that moment. Maintaining my relationship with her has been wonderful in that it's allowed me to get another side of the history of the myriad of museum professionals of color who have fought the battle against the racist culture of art museums and some who literally did lose their careers because of it.

DT: I'm wondering what you've gleaned about the individual versus collective experience and response? To what extent does something become shouldered by an individual versus a collective, and what lessons does this have for museum-related organizing?

KM: It has to be—it needs to be—collective. It wouldn't have worked if it weren't. I did have a moment last week, though, when I was livid. After Venable's resignation made the news, and it was all this celebration and "Kelli, thank you so much . . . ," I had this moment of "You don't get to say that to me because none of you said a word when I needed it seven months ago." I stand strongly in my decisions. To a large degree, this is the kind of person I am. I didn't expect people to go out on that

limb with me at that time because I know the culture—
that silence, that fear is a problem, not just in the arts
community. I knew that I was going to be alone out on
that limb. But I was pissed last week. After all I
sacrificed, after what I did . . . I did it because it needed
to be done. I spoke up because I knew no one else
would. And, to be clear, I haven't been able to find
a job since. So . . . there's that. But not working in an
institution right now is probably a good thing because
I really needed to heal and recover. The last year and
a half at Newfields was the absolute worst experience
with racism I've ever had in my life. Plus, working
independently has been a lot nicer—freer.

    Ultimately, Venable's resignation would not have
happened if it weren't for the perfect storm of many
people coming together. There were some pretty
powerful people in the city who were like, "Enough is
enough with this dude." I think the community as a
whole—because white supremacy is so normalized in
Indianapolis—was just tired. There was an upswell from
white people and people of color in Indianapolis who
were like, "We are tired of living with this weight." The
museum has been a behemoth ulcer on the larger
Indianapolis arts community for many years. That larger
community was why I was able to be there for two and a
half years.

    With this current racist job-description situation,
I think there is a little bit of guilt—you know, folks are
feeling like "Damn, we didn't help her" or "Oh, she
wasn't lying." I don't think people necessarily thought I
was lying, but I think most folks who were outside of the
museum just thought I was overreacting. Maybe feeling
like "I know it is probably bad, but it is not that bad." But
this job posting placed front and center just how bad it
really is. The wording of that posting was not a mistake.
It wasn't an oversight. It was very purposeful. When I
first saw it, before the story broke, I was like, "Oh, that's
nothing. That's just a typical day at Newfields." But the
way it horrified the nation was completely shocking
to Venable, the senior leadership, and the board. They're

        SILENCE WON'T SAVE YOU

literally that out of touch—they didn't understand why people were so upset. The entire time that they've been asserting the narratives "She was the problem," or "Kelli was just too reactionary," or "She had a terrible work ethic" around the city since my departure, they were really exposing themselves. Basically, reinforcing everything that I said with my resignation.

DT: I'm interested in your take on bigger picture questions about leadership and institutional change. Not everyone is gonna get fired and go down like Charles Venable. Not everyone who has made their employees' lives really hard and has reproduced white supremacist culture on multiple registers, whether in their exhibition making or treatment of staff, is going to go down like this. But there is maybe a taste for it and a politics around it at this point. I'm wondering what your read is on the mid-term and long-term ways in which these transitions and fights are going to play out. How does generational leadership shift?

KM: I think we have to keep our feet on their necks. We really do, because even since the uprisings of June 2020 . . . with all the letters and petitions from staff and institutions around the country—name an institution that has responded significantly and publicly. There's not a single one. I am sure there is work going on internally at a lot of institutions, but there's been no real commitment to change. The sentiment was that it was going to blow over because in the past it always has. Or people are so beat down that they're like, "Fuck it. I am going to put my head down, be quiet, and do my work."
I think we have to call out the fact that we are looking at sociopathic narcissists who are masquerading as leaders, and we need to ask how and why boards are so enamored with that. I think until we deal with the fact that boards have damn near all the money, literally nothing is going to change. A lot of those board members are the arbiters of capitalist markets. So, as a whole, the field has to change its investment in that. Funding

structures have to change. That is something I haven't figured out yet. Where do I get the money from? If I put myself, let's say, in leadership at the Met, where would I get the money from if I completely did away with the current funding model? Do we even need to be rebuilding museums? Does what we want to build need to be called something else? Can we walk away completely from the current art ecosystem and build something fresh?

I feel like if we collectively refused to work, the institutions couldn't survive. And I know that's like a pie-in-the-sky utopia kind of feeling, but it's also why I go back to collectivity. It has to be a collective effort.

DT: The problem with the way most workplace resignations that do not get media attention play out is that it doesn't ever become visible as a pattern. The most visible manifestation might be on the local job-posting board online, where you can see that a certain institution is always hiring, but you can't discern too much of a pattern beyond that.

KM: I was giving two of my former Newfields colleagues the business a couple months ago—I love them to death, and when they see this they'll know who I'm talking about, LOL—because I was like, "This is actually your battle that I'm fighting, because you should have said something when you left!" The reason I always talk about speaking out is because we leave, we go to the next place, and it happens all over again. It's such a vicious cycle that it is basically normalized. And institutions have very strategic ways of covering up that truth to keep the cycle going.

Over the last six months, I've spoken to so many curators and museum professionals who've said one of three things: "I've left the field," or "I'm working independently," or "I've found a place where it's tolerable." Meaning, "I've found a place where I don't feel like I'm selling my soul every day."

And I've thought to myself, "How are cultural workers feeling like that in museums? This ain't the CIA.

SILENCE WON'T SAVE YOU

We ain't torturing people in a back room somewhere. This is artwork." But the more I think about it, the more I considered the legacy and vestiges of colonization and imperialism upon which museums rest, and I literally said to myself, "OMG Kelli! No, it's not a hot war, but it absolutely is a space where culture wars are located, carried out, and literally preserved!" I think we really have to speak honestly about that. Until we reckon with that collectively as a field, the problems will continue recreating themselves over and over again.

This interview took place on February 26, 2021. Thank you to Hal Martin for this transcription.

PANDEMIC BOOKKEEPING

Cheryl Derricotte

My new series, Pandemic Bookkeeping, shares an assessment of how I stack up against the standards set for those who ran Victorian and Civil War–era middle-class households, standards that still haunt us today. Images from the 1861 British classic *Mrs. Beaton's Book of Household Management* are layered upon blank pages from Clara Barton's contemporaneous journal. While Isabella Beaton devoted herself to home and husband, Barton was a revered Civil War nurse, often traveling with the Union Army, and is best known as the founder of the American Red Cross.

 It is not lost on me that, according to these standards, I would occupy the position of a servant on either side of the Atlantic "pond" in the 1860s. During the COVID-19 pandemic, I often felt like I had woken up in a Dickens novel or in the middle of the Civil War. And yet, today, like many women, I am required to embody both Clara and Isabella: a focused career woman (serving society) and a goddess of domesticity (maintaining understated beauty and a well-appointed home). Like it or not, I also occupy the precariously demanding positions of mistress, housekeeper, and cook. Clearly, I have enough bed pillows, but, really, only two demitasse spoons? This is my plague journal. I am counting.

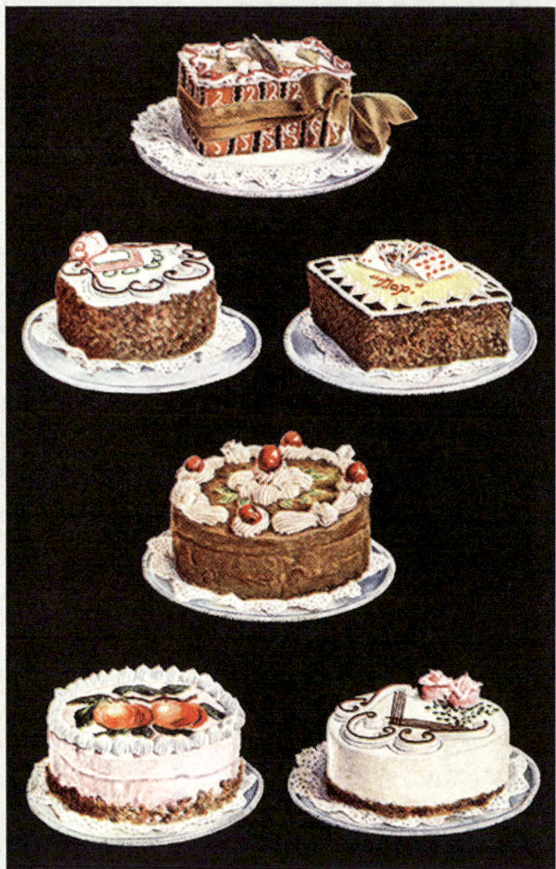

Cakes and Gâteaux showing various styles of Icing and Decoration.

lbs, flour	5
tins of baking powder	2
yeast packets	3
lb powdered sugar	1

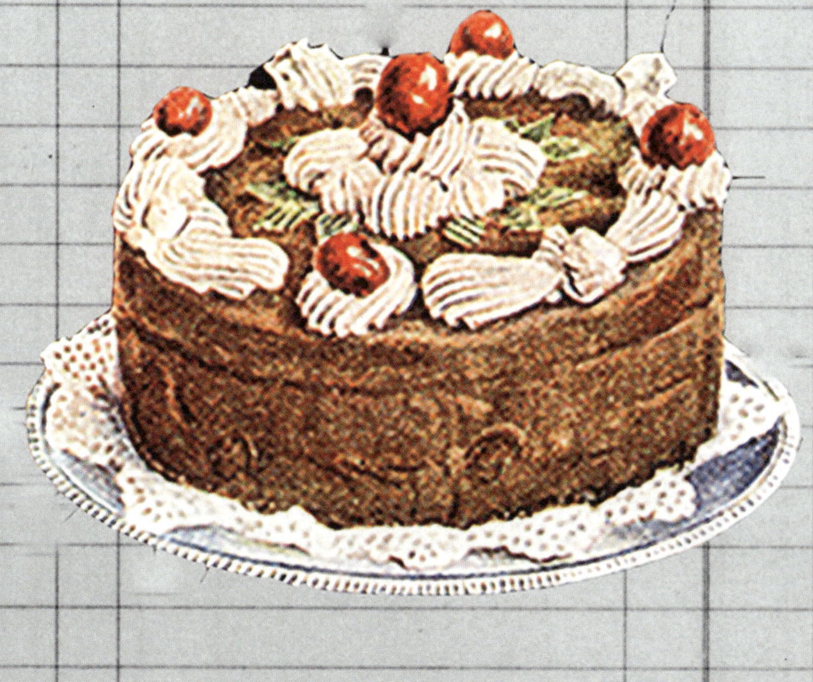

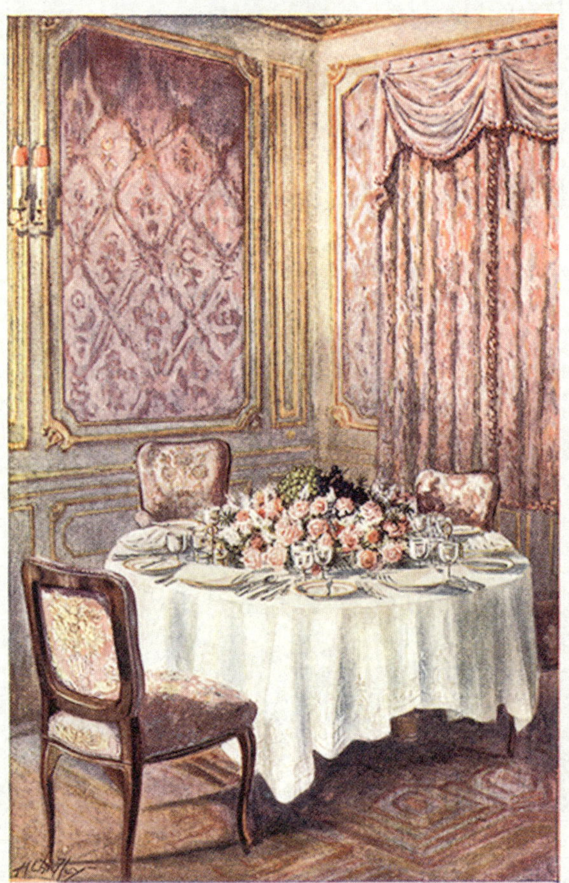

DINNER TABLE.

The floral decorations are kept low to facilitate conversation.

plates	4
glasses	8
cloth napkins	4
demitasse spoons	2

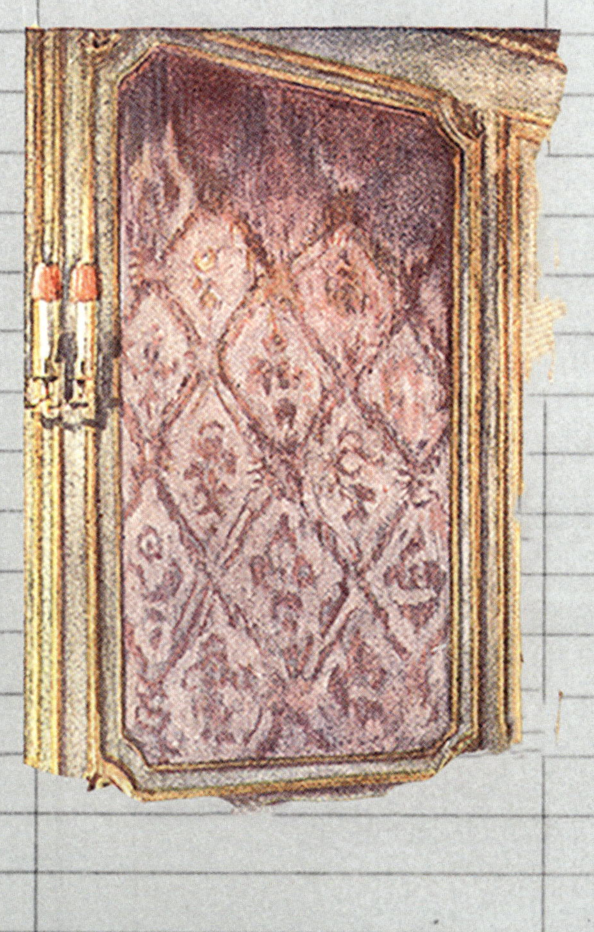

peaches 6
bunches/grapes I

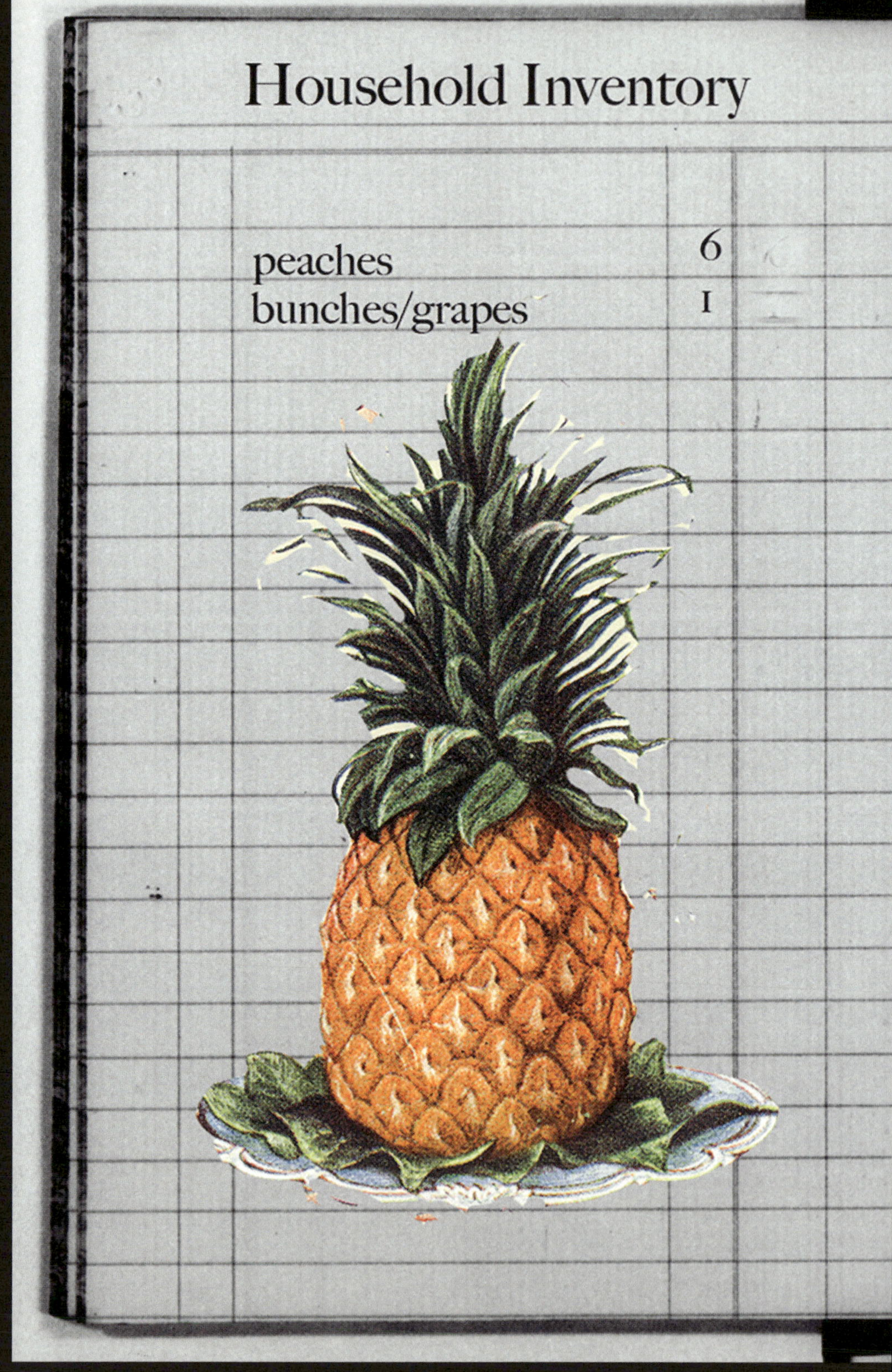

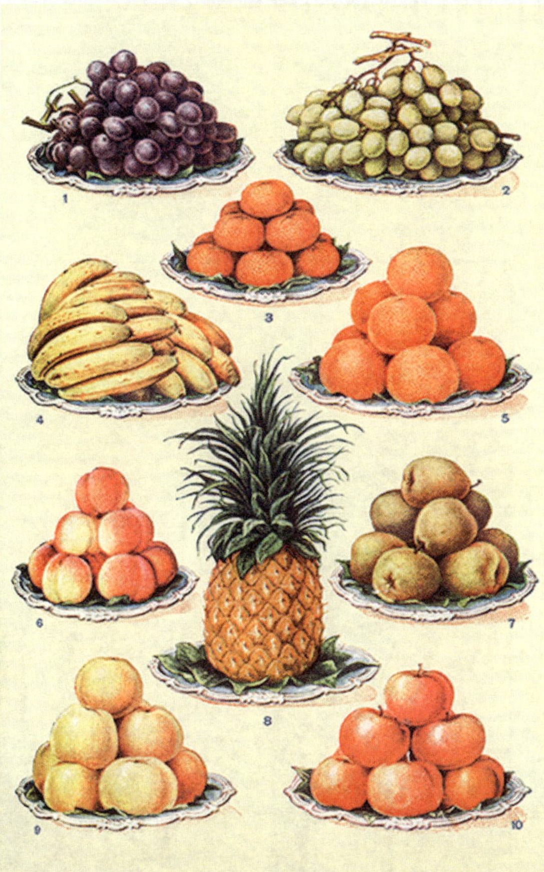

DESSERT FRUIT.
1—Black Grapes.   2—Muscat Grapes.   3—Tangerines.   4—Bananas.   5—Oranges.
6—Peaches.   7—Pears.   8—Pineapple.   9 and 10—Apples.
GG

Household Inventory

sheet sets		3		
cotton blankets		2		

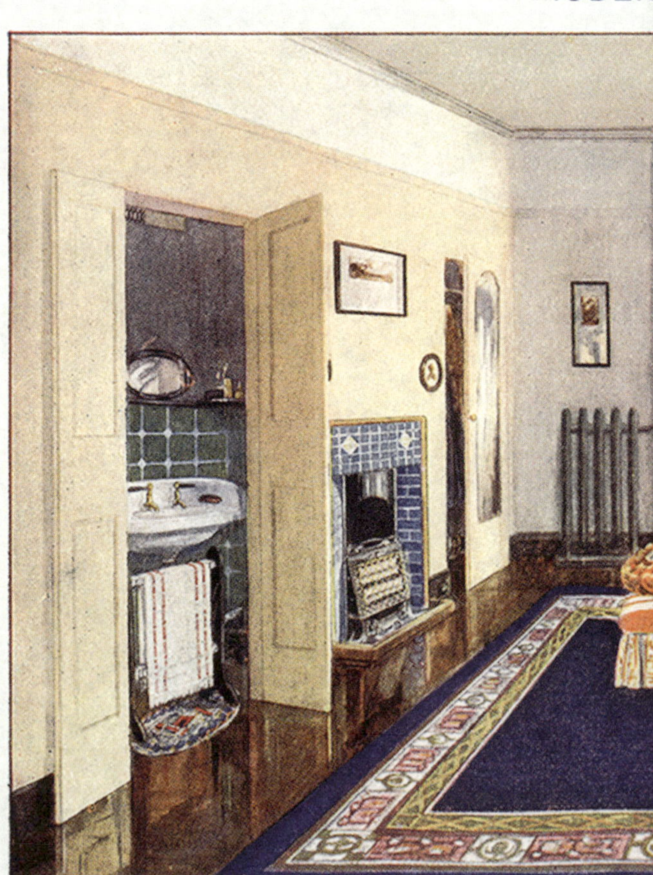

There are no unnecessary shelves or mouldings on which dus
space, and the wash-basin is enclosed by doors to el

| pillows | 4 |
| down alternative comforters | 2 |

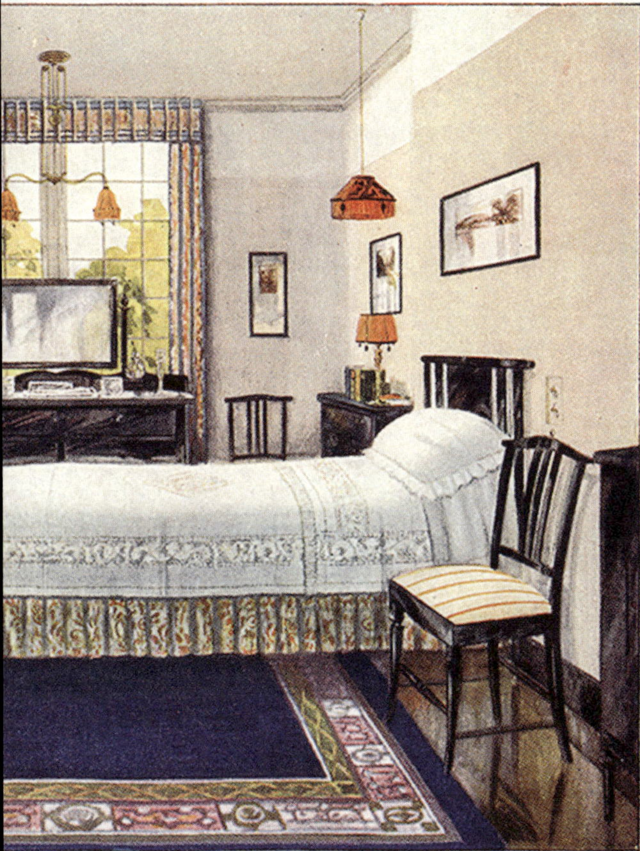

collect. The wardrobe is "built into" the wall to economise
ll danger from noxious gases from the waste pipe.

Household Inventory

	flower vases	2
	wine glasses	8
	table cloths	3

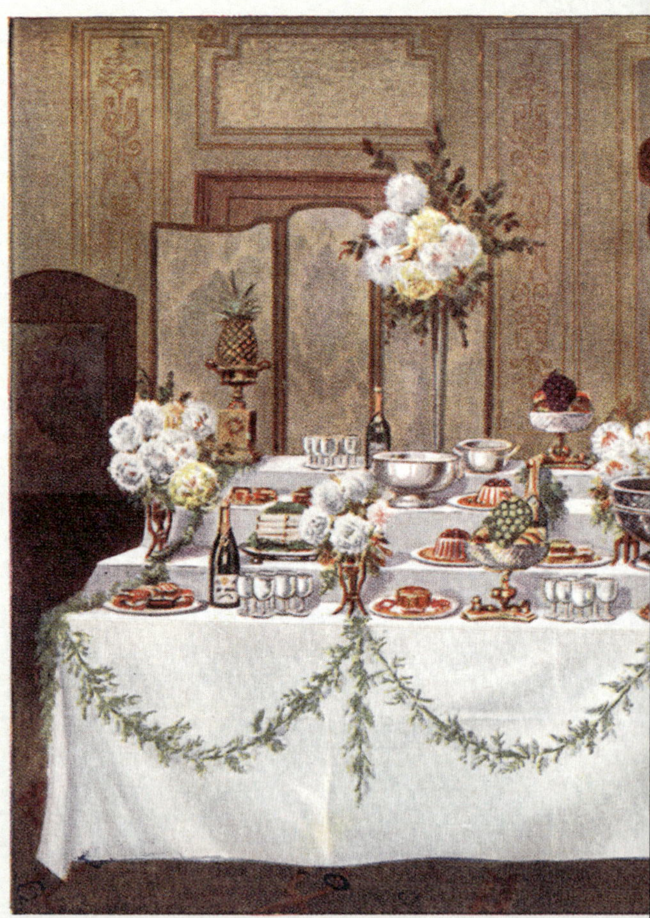

champagne flutes	8
serving bowls	2
buffet platters	1

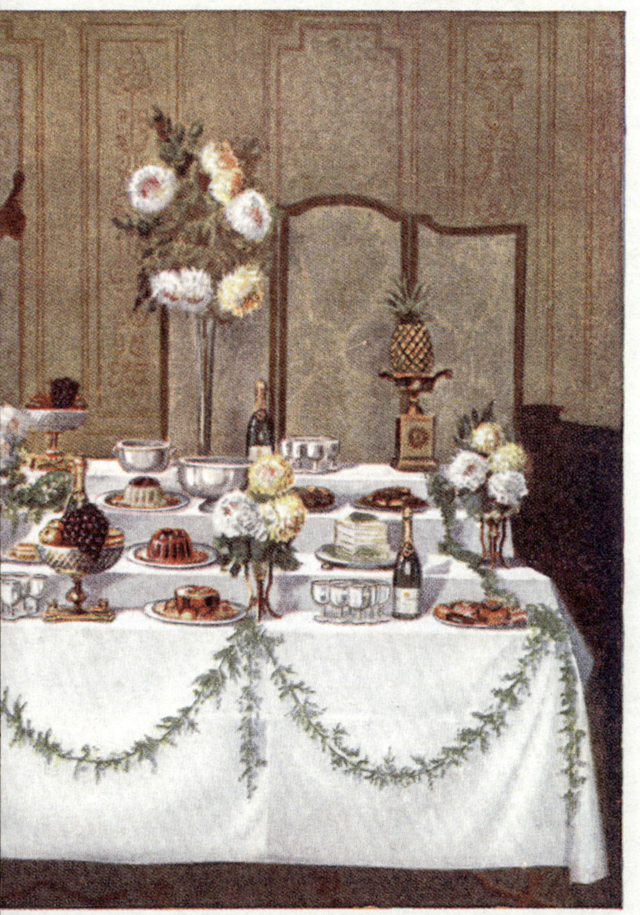

Household Inventory

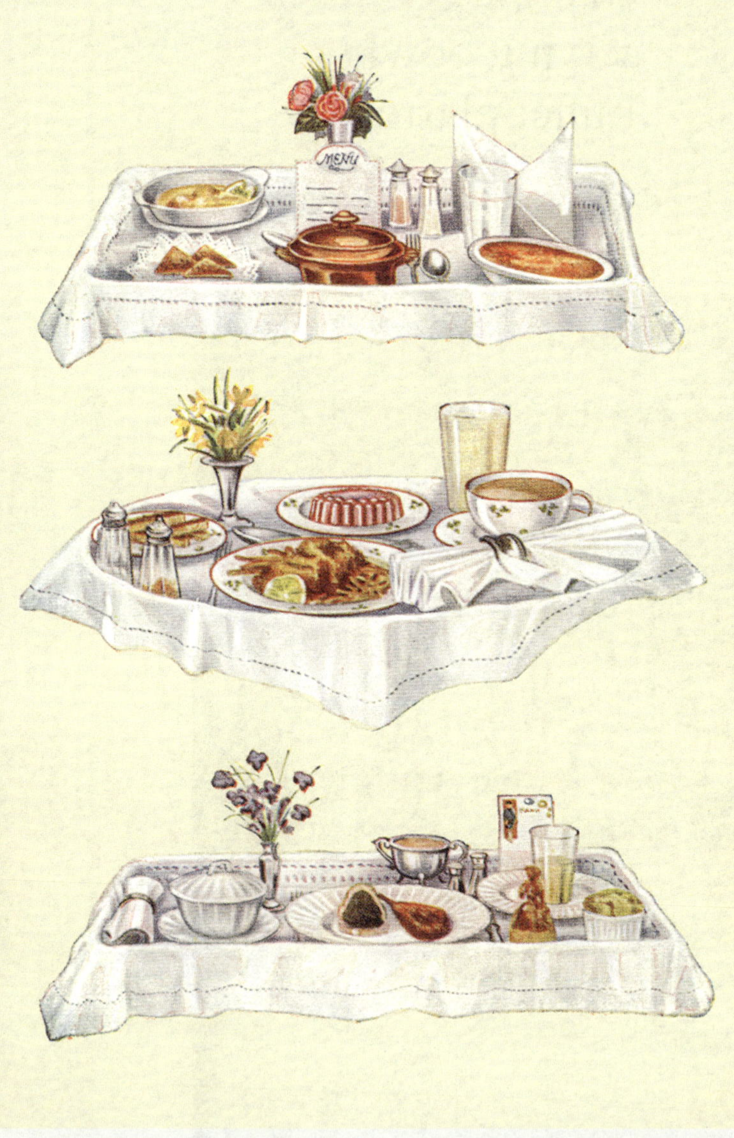

1—Steamed Fillets of Sole, Fairy Toast, Beef Tea, Baked Custard, Barley Water.
2—Toast, Fried Soles and Potato Straws, Beef Tea, Lemonade, Jelly.
3—Clear Soup, Lamb Cutlet. Mashed Potato and Spinach, Milanaise Soufflé,
Lemonade, Tomato Sauce.

QQ

October 13, 2020

bud vases	1
juice glasses	4
small plates	4
cotton napkins	8
soup bowls	4

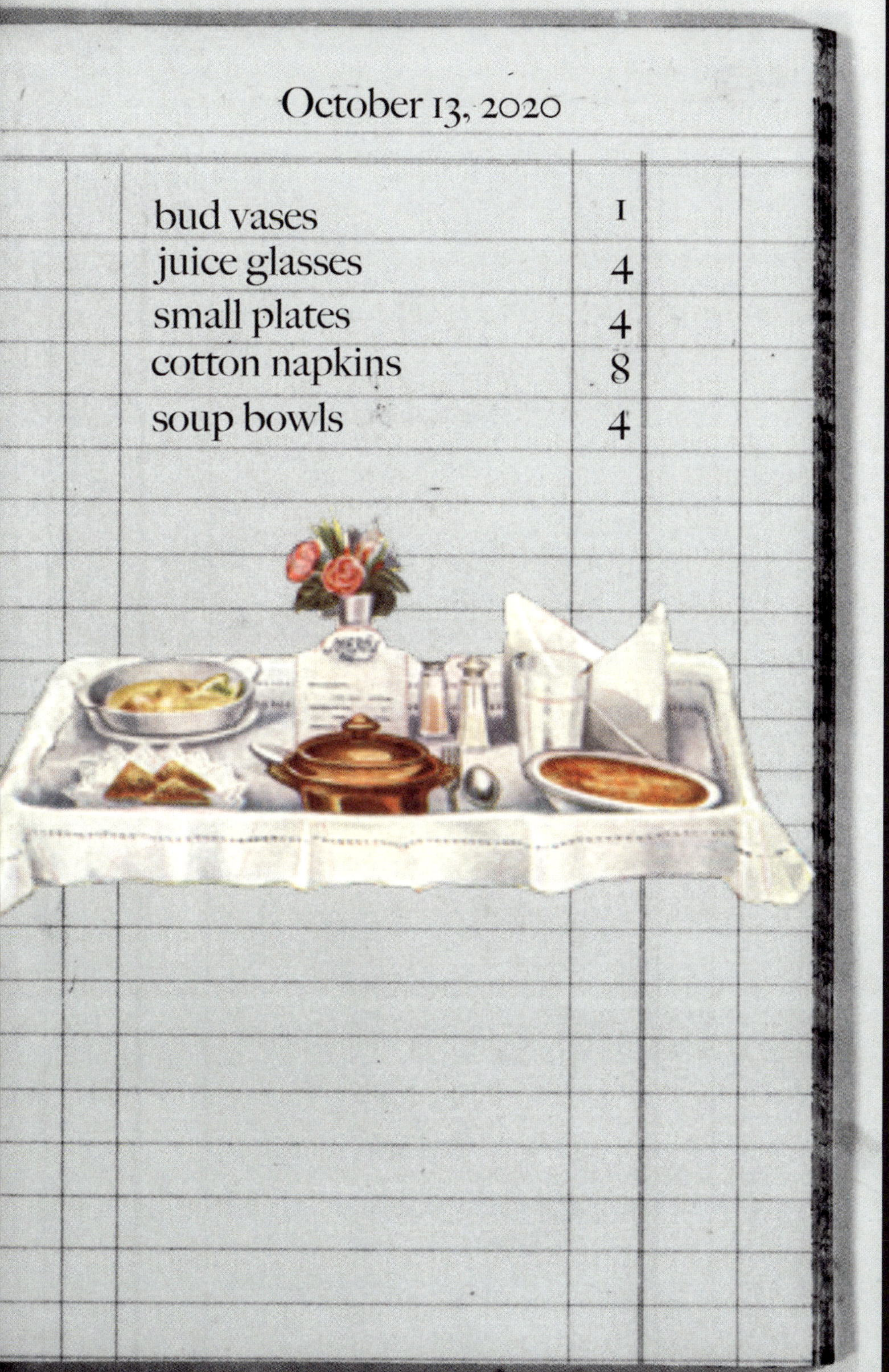

ENLIGHTENMENT OF COLOR

Dan S. Wang

I see Black people adopting Buddhist meditation and chanting, meet Latinx folks finding appeal in the dharma, read about Native Americans putting their spiritual practices in conversation with Buddhist precepts and cosmologies, and I join with Asian Americans asserting primacy in the narrative of Buddhism in the United States. These developments amount to a racial diversification of American Buddhism, a major tradition label under which there exists a constellation of spiritual communities. Many have noted that until pretty recently much of the higher-visibility segments of the American Buddhist landscape were nearly all white. Having had a lifelong, if not always a disciplined, engagement with Buddhism, through dual streams of conversion and heritage, I offer reflections on this ever-so-slight turning.

My observations are casual, unscientific, and without a perspective from inside an organization or formal body. Be that as it may, from a ground-level view I have seen that in only a few years, my options for practicing meditation in sangha with people of color (POC), either exclusively or primarily, have grown from none to several. As of this writing in the summer of 2021, I know of at least five or six POC-centered sitting groups in Los Angeles; I have attended four of them myself. Considering that Southern California has long

1

For this essay I choose to use the abbreviation POC for the category of "people of color" rather than the more differentiated abbreviation BIPOC, which stands for "Black, Indigenous, People of Color." I use BIPOC in other writing, but not in this one for a number of reasons: chief among them being that the essay does not hinge on a politics of differentiation to the extent that the full term "Black, Indigenous, People of Color" serves no purpose in this text. Instead, I specify groups, populations, and communities where necessary.

2

Rima Vesely-Flad, *Black Buddhists and the Black Radical Tradition: The Practice of Stillness in the Movement for Liberation* (New York: NYU Press, 2021); Chenxing Han, *Be the Refuge: Raising the Voices of Asian American Buddhists* (Berkeley: North Atlantic Books, 2021).

3

Sangha is a Sanskrit term meaning the community of Buddhist practitioners or, more generically, one's group of fellow seekers. Such is the importance of sangha that it is considered one of the Three Jewels, along with the dharma and the Buddha himself.

4

"Religious Landscape Study," Pew Research Center, accessed February 2021, pewforum.org/religious-landscape-study/.

been home to the country's most concentrated population of Buddhists outside of Hawaii, the newness of POC sanghas speaks to the historical racial homogeneity of American Buddhism and, with respect to the long-established temples and organizations of various immigrant Asian origins, how mutually segregated the Buddhist landscape has been.[1]

While undoubtedly touched with an urgency corresponding to the resurgent movement for racial justice following the murder of George Floyd, and the subsequent pattern of American institutions conducting an overdue reckoning with racial disparities and injustice, this rise in interest also feels as if a slow-brewing change has finally broken the surface. New books published in 2021 indicate as much: Rima Vesely-Flad's forthcoming *Black Buddhists and the Black Radical Tradition: The Practice of Stillness in the Movement for Liberation* and Chenxing Han's *Be the Refuge: Raising the Voices of Asian American Buddhists*, which became available in the spring, just in time for me to binge on it while writing this essay.[2] It seemed that every couple of months in the first year of the pandemic I would hear about another talk on a topic related to POC and Buddhism, some of which attracted sizable streaming audiences. The main thing is that there are now more and more ways for POC practitioners to connect with each other. The rainbow sangha has emerged.[3]

Sangha and Composition

While I am eminently unqualified to answer them, my questions about POC in Buddhism are many. First among them: What meaning is to be found in the uptick in POC self-identifying as Buddhist? Surveys of religious attitudes and practices in the US show that there is a decline in membership in Christian denominations of all types, that those claiming no religion are the fastest growing group, and that Buddhism is the only major religion drawing an increasing number of adherents.[4]

154

A growing presence of POC in Buddhism makes sense as a reflection of a nation diversifying as a whole. But, apart from the general trend toward an increasingly diverse America, and given the social conditions with which different POC contend and considering what Buddhist practices and philosophy offer adherents, I find the racial diversification of American Buddhism intriguing as a space with the potential to mix different liberation traditions.

What are the patterns at play? Though growing, Buddhists are a very small slice of the entire American religious landscape: by most measures less than 1 percent of the overall population. While historically and presently most concentrated in California and Hawaii, their presence is national; directories list scores of temples, organizations, and centers across all fifty states. Ever increasingly, POC-only groups are springing up both within and outside of these networks, but are some of the new patterns in keeping with earlier phases of American Buddhism? Within the broad category of Buddhism, there are groups founded according to different schools of practice along with those that are purposefully ecumenical. Additionally, the full range of Buddhisms includes the organizations bearing self-titled ethnic or culturally specific identities (e.g., Khmer, Korean, or Viet).

Buddhism in the United States collects under one heading possibly the most diverse range of Buddhist lineages to be found in any national context. Considering this variety, I wonder, who are these newer practitioners of color and to what lineages are they drawn? By what avenues do they enter into Buddhist practice and philosophy? Are the faces of color one sees in today's increasingly mixed sangha similar in class profile to the earlier generations of white and Jewish bohemians and intellectuals who latched onto Buddhism as a departure from their own religious starting points? POC Buddhist practitioners and sanghas may be growing, but are they as diverse as the big tent implies? Are American converts to Zen, Tibetan, and Theravadan practice less white than they used to be—but still elite? That is, do the increasingly visible Black adherents and teachers in Vipassanā sanghas hail from upper-middle-class worlds, either through family of origin or of their own making, and enjoy the benefits of higher education and/or professional status? If so, then perhaps the emerging racial diversity within American Buddhism mirrors the class dynamics at play in the larger society, in which the resource-rich worlds of elite education and professional life are, by design, more racially mixed than some of the persistently segregated worlds of the less privileged.

What about the "push" factors, the tensions between oneself and the faith of one's upbringing that drive one into a seeking mode? Atheistic doubt would be an obvious point of contention for those questioning the Christianity, Judaism, or Islam they were born into. The noted overrepresentation of queer and non-binary practitioners of color suggests that patriarchal attitudes play some role in LGBTQI people having a reason to look beyond, say, an inherited conservative tradition. Whatever the inadequacies of other religions that contribute to these trends of lapsed membership, it stands to reason that Buddhism, with its variable theism across different schools of thought and its secular corollaries in mindful-ness practices, would gain adherents. Considering Buddhism's capacity for coexistence with other traditions, a phenomenon of complementarity seen repeatedly throughout history as Buddhism expanded outside of its area of origin, the gain is on some level unsurprising. In the US context, coming to Buddhism from a Black church tradition, for example, one may not feel the need to choose between them. And heritage practitioners of Indigenous religions may come to understand Buddhism as a complementary tradition rather than an invasive competitor.

What about Asian Americans? Is Buddhism not Asian to begin with? Yes, but that does not mean much. "Asian American" is already a massively unwieldy category for the purposes of typology. Here, there is the added historical complication of the dharma's having emerged in today's Northern India and migrated through different Asian societies, much as one could say that Christianity came out of what is, in the latest parlance, West Asia. Buddhism traveled an incredible passage of Asian geographies and societies, all of which presented different social conditions. Buddhism interacted with other major traditions, sometimes resulting in mutual influence, and found residence in all kinds of social orders before spreading across world geographies. The earliest Buddhist communities in the US were established by Japanese and Chinese immigrant groups arriving in successive waves beginning more than 150 years ago.

So, when I ponder today's widening encounter of POC and Buddhism, am I even thinking of Asian Americans? Well, yes, even though in aggregate Asians have long accounted for a majority of Buddhists in the US, because some Asian Americans, just like Black and white practitioners, travel a Buddhist journey not as an inheritance but as an adoption, discovery, and conversion. Asian Americans run the gamut in terms of experiences, from being raised attending Buddhist temples that overlap with their ethnic particularity to discovering the dharma as a meaningful alternative to, say, the evangelical Christianity of their parents. As with political leanings and household income, the extreme range of Asian American pathways to the dharma shows nothing conclusive except the limitations of "Asian American" as a demographic category.

As often happens in higher education, corporate staffing, the art world, and other contexts, in the sphere of American Buddhism there may be a stubborn gap between what we imagine and desire as "diversity" and the actualized diversity of composition, wherein, for example, patterns of gender composition shift toward inclusion but race and/or class composition do not, or the converse. "Partial diversities" may be the most available, and this should be remembered when either lauding or criticizing the still-emerging trends.[5]

5

While corporate and institutional bodies jumped on the diversity-equity-inclusion bandwagon in the wake of the George Floyd Uprising, offering a spectrum of responses ranging from issuing statements to initiating internal reviews to promising new cluster hires, of course it remains to be seen what results may come. Buddhist organizations have done likewise. Without the corporate or governmental resources to reallocate or redirect, backing up statements with action will be somewhat different for them. An example of doing what they can is this acknowledgment and resource page issued by *Tricycle*, a leading journal of popular Buddhism in the US that has in the past been criticized for dismissing the concerns of Asian American practitioners. See "Addressing Violence Against Asian Americans," *Tricycle*, March 19, 2021, https://tricycle.org/ trikedaily/aapi-hate/.

Particularity and *Śūnyatā*

Apart from the question of composition, does the recognition of POC particularity—historically grounded as it is—run counter to the idealized universality of the dharma? Does our contemporary understanding of identity complement or conflict with a 2,500-year-old tradition that has migrated and mutated all along, while crossing countless political borders? Rarely, if ever, deliberate in the negation of other major traditions, Buddhisms—plural—have insinuated themselves meaningfully into the spiritual and social fabric of dozens of ethnic, linguistic, and national formations, often in coexistence with other religions, and into the cultural life of scores of localized contexts. Social difference has not been an obstacle to the spread of Buddhism.

These questions are especially important because of the honesty they demand of us. Pinpointing how and where our particularity—in my case, Chinese American—locates us in the social web goes to the heart of contemporary identity consciousness. As a social and political construction that is historically contingent, one might argue that such consciousness makes legible the pain and suffering that come from the *this-worldly* subjugation to an often brutal racial hierarchy. This is the kind of suffering inflicted by concrete circumstances of violence and deprivation, engineered under the auspices of a political arrangement. But a corresponding political liberation does not necessarily address the strictures of human existence that are not defined by historical and political circumstances. Suffering exists outside of material deprivation and state violence, which is to say, outside of history, too.

Does, therefore, the promise of universal enlightenment exist beyond the horizon of identity formation? If so, perhaps the challenge before POC practitioners is to cultivate a wisdom capable of discerning what of our suffering is historically constituted and what of it exists outside of history (i.e., what of it is universal to all human beings). This, I sense, may be the *prajna,*

   ENLIGHTENMENT OF COLOR

the deep understanding, toward which the new wave of POC Buddhists travel on a dharma journey, whether that be in accordance with the Threefold Training, the Eightfold Path, or the many other regimens of concerted practice—or the rather more casual practice of dharma-informed everyday mindfulness, compassion, and wisdom.

For so many POC in the United States, the apprehension of *śūnyatā*—that void permeating all of reality that is too often translated for convenience as "emptiness," that abyss into which meaning may fall without ever landing, revealed by the impermanence of our daily existence—is terribly fraught. For what are we without our historically constituted suffering, our experience of oppression? If the Buddha's most basic piece of wisdom is that pain is a product of attachment, an insight worked over in countless ways by thousands of masters and millions of dharma practitioners over the centuries, for many POC in the contemporary United States, one's pain can easily become its own attachment, particularly when our political power is made to rest on our moral authority as hurt and aggrieved democratic subjects. In other words, an *attachment* to the pain produced by the circumstances of subjugation to a racist, imperialist society that captures us in its political subjecthood can be another source of pain. And yet, all of history is nothing if not essentially impermanent, always changing and ever in motion. And that includes systems of oppression, exploitation, and inequality. The most mighty of empires can and *will* fall. Our social and political engagement is founded on the very belief that conditions do change and that no edifice, no matter how grand or terrible or seemingly supreme, is forever. Attaining a state of acceptance of, shall we say, a "*śūnyatā* of color" bears the promise of that most alluring and yet frightening turns of mind: a mode of self-regard that overflows the restrictions of our historical oppression, a mental event horizon beyond which we see ourselves as fully human, perhaps for the first time.

Could the application of Zen, Vipassana, and other traditions of Buddhist practice by Black people to the contemporary and particular conditions of Black suffering be a transmission—faith taking a leap, as it were—as momentous as that of, say, D. T. Suzuki's delivery of the dharma to American audiences in the 1950s? Suzuki introduced his interpretations of Zen philosophy and practice to white-dominated audiences in Europe and the United States at a time of growing unease having to do with destructive technologies, political disillusionment, and accelerating social change. The seemingly self-satisfied society produced no shortage of seekers. In the decades that followed, enough converts committed to the various dharma schools to establish in aggregate what many scholars now term Western Buddhism. As Western Buddhism diversifies to the degree that Black people and other POC bring their various spiritual heritages into a deep cultural exchange with Buddhism, the potential combination of wisdoms is a tantalizing possibility.

In present times, the contradictions between our values and our reality overwhelm us. The hydrocarbon economy must be undone, and, yet, even minimal participation in society entails reproducing it. With unprecedented drama, COVID-19 has proven humanity to be a single biological family, but in response, governments have strengthened borders instead of dismantling them. And, for POC in particular, our work of decolonial world building is vexed by an internal impasse: that of an identity awareness that empowers but also seriously limits. Given such conditions, I wonder if a turn toward Buddhist philosophy and practice presents people of color with a path back to the universal, but one that overrides the pseudo-universalisms of European Enlightenment that bequeathed the terms under which we struggle politically. Instead, dharma practices can trace existential paths from any particular starting point of suffering, bringing the timeless challenges of life and death to bear on our profane and too often all-consuming concerns.

Thus I take heart when, for example, African American biracial Zen priest Angel Kyodo Williams maps the Three Jewels of Buddhism onto the everyday coping strategies of contemporary Black life—and in the process demonstrates the availability of emancipation through the dharma for people of all races and ethnicities. Or when Asian American author and renowned Insight meditation teacher Larry Yang directly addresses the intertwined social separations that prevent the universal message of the dharma from reaching those who may benefit most. This goes against the long-prevailing colorblindness of predominantly white sanghas, out of which some voices intensified an erasure of POC perspectives by leaning into a universalism that depends on a seeking subject with no worldly profile, with no race or gender, for its usefulness. And I think of when Black journalist Dani McClain speaks of a breathing and stillness practice, and of Buddhist principles in relation to her memories of her grandmother, who used to tell her, when asked why she was sleeping during the day, "I'm not sleeping, I'm resting my eyes." That is when I hear the tradition evolving with bottom-up richness. These voices, and an expanding network of similarly engaged POC practitioners, indicate an evolution, an enlargement of POC self-recognition, toward an openness to the Four Noble Truths—(1) life is painful, (2) attachment is the cause of our pain, (3) there is a way to free ourselves from attachment, and (4) the Eightfold Path points the way—but from the experience of those subject to historically contingent circumstances of oppression.[6]

A Stream of Breath

Where and how do artists figure in? I wonder specifically about POC artists in the US, of which of course I am one. I am not necessarily thinking of artists who make representations of mindfulness, meditation, the dharma, or anything identifiably Buddhist (though they might). Nor am I wondering about artists who create so-called contemplative work or use contemplative processes.

6
Angel Kyodo Williams, *Being Black: Zen and the Art of Living with Fearlessness and Grace* (New York: Penguin Compass, 2000); Larry Yang, *Awakening Together: The Spiritual Practice of Inclusivity and Community* (Somerville: Wisdom Publications, 2017); adrienne marie brown, "Basically for Being a Human Being: Meditation with Dani McClain," in *Emergent Strategy: Shaping Change, Changing Worlds* (Chico, CA: AK Press, 2017), 179.

I am thinking of artists who *have* a Buddhist practice, as opposed to artists who make Buddhist art. I know of a few, which means there must be more. Two contributed to this volume, Sandra de la Loza and Cheryl Derricotte. Neither could be said to make art that foregrounds Buddhist motifs, dharma messages, or contemplative purpose. For both, their engagement with the Buddhist tradition is founded primarily on breath-driven sitting and other ways of using meditative stillness to complement their lives as makers of art. For example, though Derricotte occasionally makes use of Buddhist imagery in her glass work, her spiritual practice often comes into her studio as breath-rests. When wrestling with difficult topics, for example the traumas of police brutality, she says, "If I get overwhelmed with the gravity of the subject matter, short meditations help me stay present to making the work and not falling into despair." It is an inner cultivation that runs parallel to these artists' publicly engaged art making. As such, the role of Buddhism in their creative lives is quite different than the Zen stream of experimentation familiar to students of art history (i.e., the narrative of John Cage and his artistic descendants). Unlike the Cageian obsession with the incorporation of indeterminacy and suspension of judgement into art forms, practitioners like de la Loza and Derricotte begin with the body and breathing emphases of the Theravadan schools so as to continue their topical work. As a rough typology of sourcing, one could say that the Cageian approach derives from the teachings of Suzuki while the new POC Buddhism mostly springs out of schools of thought popularly associated with Thích Nhất Hạnh.

Whatever this new age of Lastgaspism is—perhaps for completeness let's call it the George Floyd Pandemic Anthropocene—little is clear but the essential truths: water is life, breath is life. When the oppressions of climate injustice, racism, and poverty choke individuals, endanger whole classes of people, and destabilize ecosystems and the atmosphere itself, the simple act of breathing takes on liberatory potential. Because we are

ENLIGHTENMENT OF COLOR

trapped in these systems even as we profess opposing values and contribute to movements of resistance, real liberation means not only abolishing external forces of oppression but transforming our internal patterns of thinking, feeling, and being. Emancipate yourself from mental slavery, the prophet Marcus Garvey spoke. We all know that is easier said than done. A Buddhist corollary would be: seek enlightenment and an escape from *samsara*, the endless cycle of suffering. Given the interlocked and potentially terminal crises at this moment in history, the stakes never have been higher. But the connection between breath and enlightenment is not new; the fact of *dukkha*—pain—in its forms of loss, despair, and loneliness is as ancient as human life itself. Though little more than a rumor, the turn to the dharma on the part of artists of color bodes well for what comes after the end times: an inhalation, a first gasp.

FIVE THESES TOWARD A GATHERING OF BIG BROWN

Karthik Pandian and
Anthony Romero

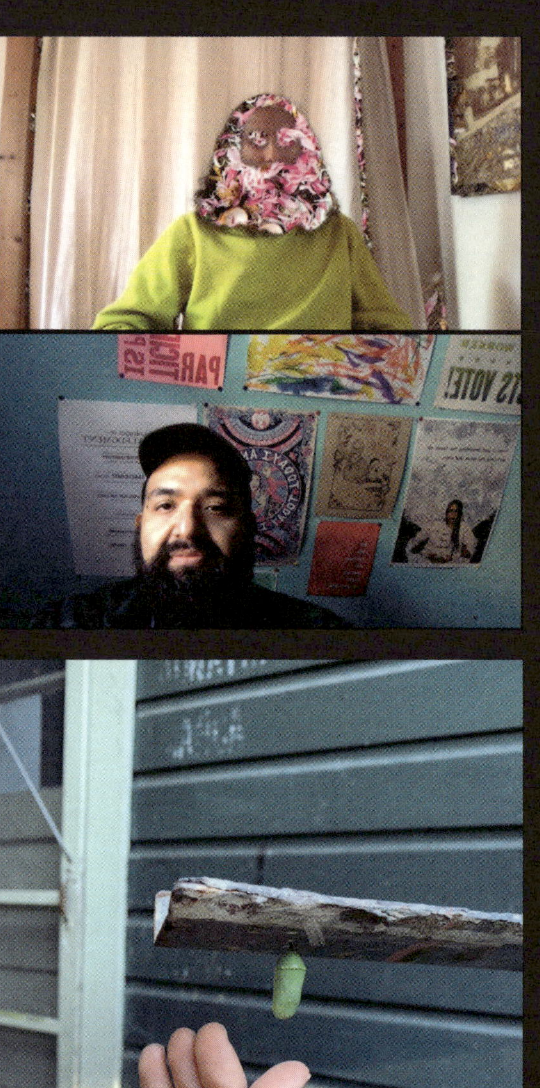

FIVE THESES TOWARD A GATHERING OF BIG B

1.

Big Brown is the practice of care-
full misrecognition.

To brown, ours and yours, what is
there to say other than to express
our collective desire to be together?
Still and moving. To find a place to
exclude ourselves. To linger there.
To arrange on the patchy grass
under the dappled light, our bodies
in a picnic of language. We babble
the words, taking pleasure in resting
together, in agreement, laughter,
and kinship—still, but always moving
toward one another, toward the
horizon of excess, toward becoming
too much, unsatisfying the gaze that
seeks to recognize us. If, once or
twice, or a thousand and one times,
we were asked where we were from,
fixed in place, made whole, pinned
to a map on this or that side of the
border, we are now shaping and
being shaped by our communion,
remaking ourselves from the
overflow of identification into an
abundant we. A "we" that we call Big
Brown . . . at least for now.

Karthik Pandian and Anthony Romero

2.

Big Brown is the feeling of
forgetting brown.

To brown, we have been with you,
beside you, been you. Untroubled
stares travel our skin. We have felt
the technology of the gaze peel us,
place us, break us by making us
whole. We too have been turned to
stone, broken. We have felt ourselves
discovered, mapped, abandoned,
evicted, and sent back to the wrong
address, the wrong body, the wrong
name. Big Brown is the feeling of
collectively forgetting the feeling of
having been brown to begin with. It
is loving being broken together.
Dissolving into one another. Breaking
into laughter, breaking into tears,
breaking into our bodies. Big Brown
laughs with our wrongness, loves
our incompleteness, and sheds
belonging, reveling in the affection
of belligerence.

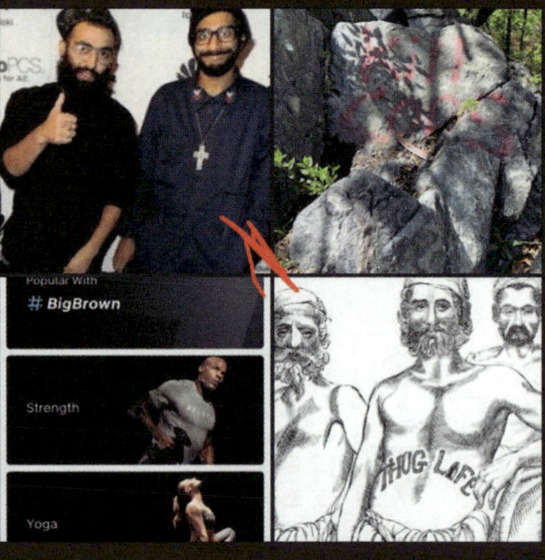

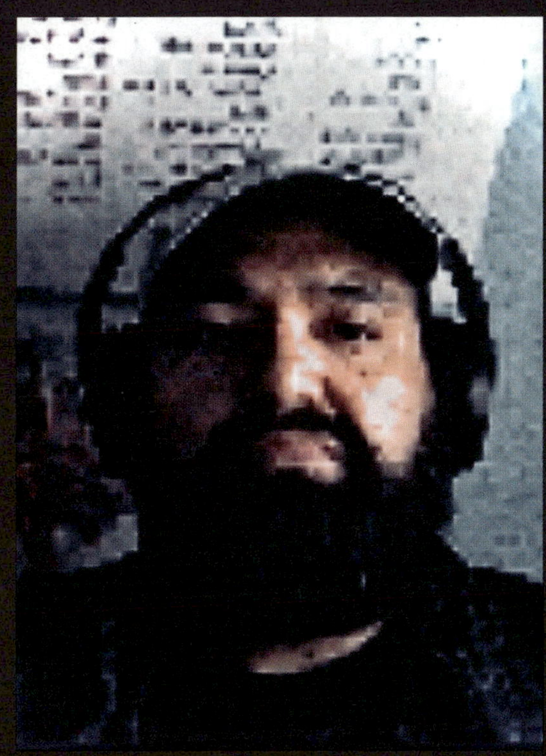

Karthik Pandian and Anthony Romero

Big Brown incompletes the gaze
that seeks to fix it.

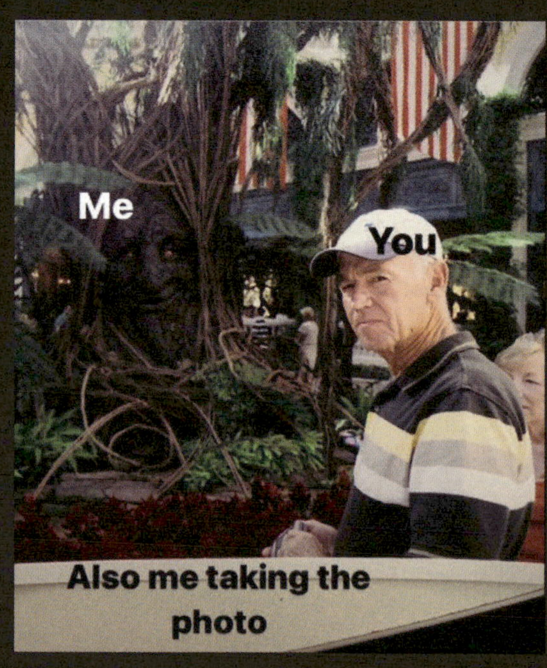

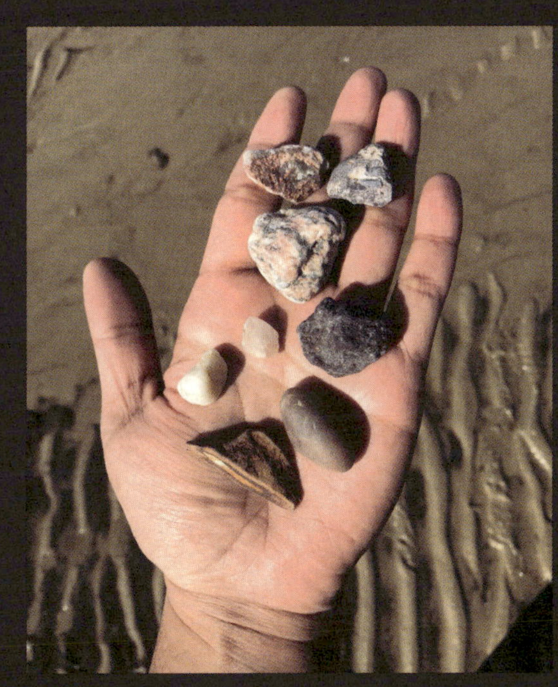

Karthik Pandian and Anthony Romero

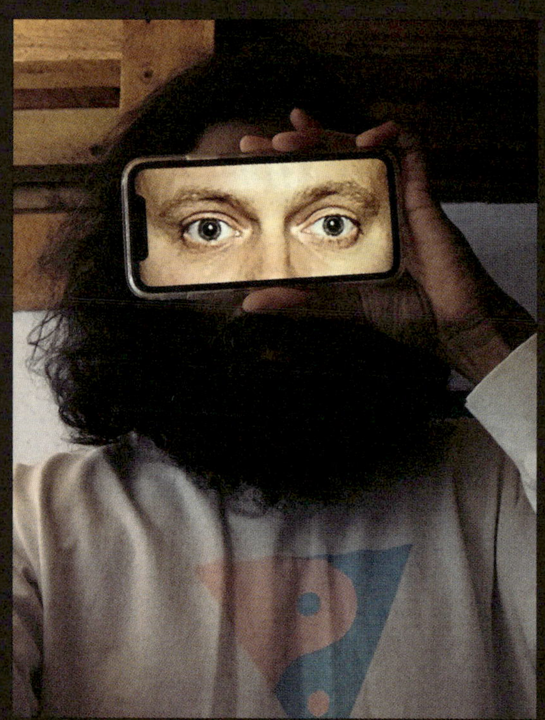

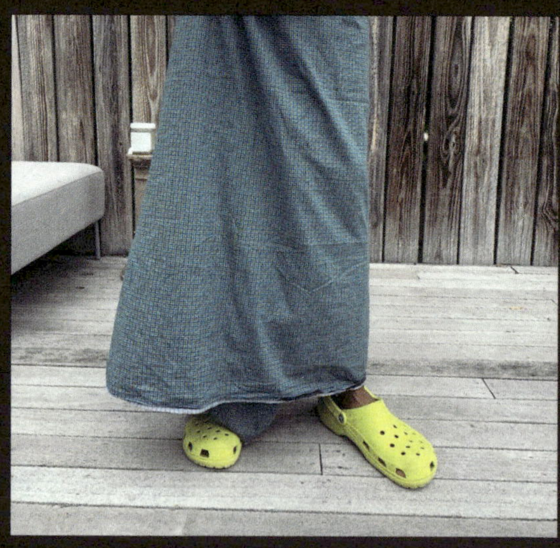

FIVE THESES TOWARD A GATHERING OF BIG BROWN

4.

Big Brown is in front of and behind, before and after.

To brown, surrounded. Know that preparations are being made. Tables set. Knives sharpened. Beards oiled. There is no need to pack since we've always been packed. If anything, we are virtuosic packers. There will be no orderly lines, no nothing in our pockets, no stepping aside this time. We are not organizing. No registration is required. No papers. Forge a napkin from your documents. We will not verify you. We will not convince you, because Big Brown is not an argument. It is a nod. A waggle. An entwined route. Big Brown is not liberation; it is relaxation along the path. It is the energy we feel when we are together. Together, we stunt past the edge of brown. Together, we feel free.

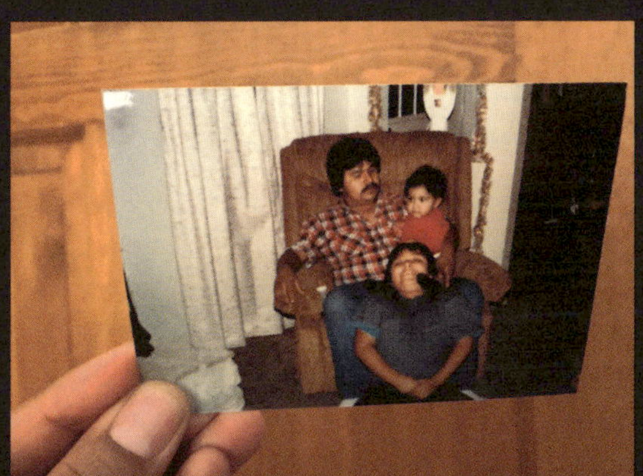

Big Brown leaves togethe

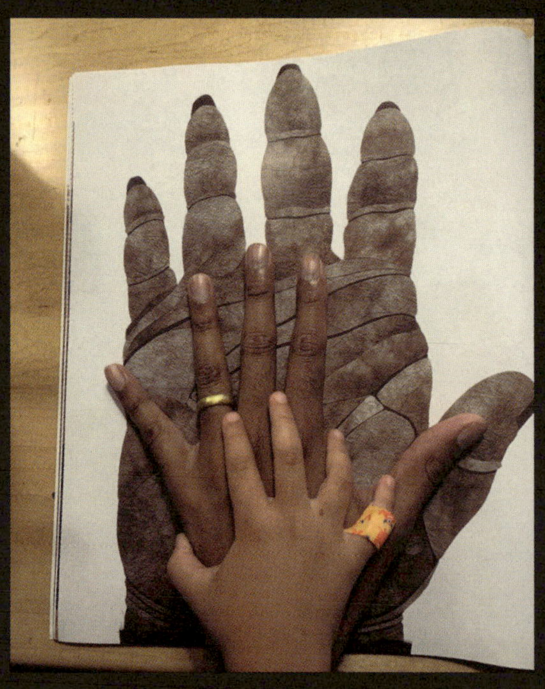

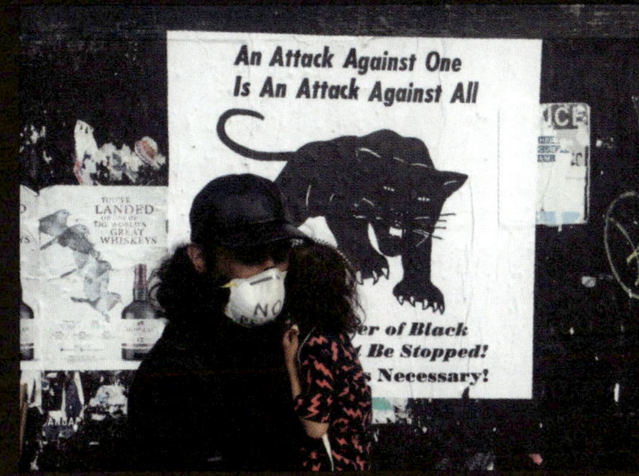

Karthik Pandian and Anthony Romero

AFTERMATH

Kimberly Bain

One

You remember, don't you? Edward Crawford throwing the tear gas canister. You must: it was August 2014, in the eighty-degree heat of late summer. The news of the stalking, threatening, choking, and murder of Michael Brown by Ferguson police officer Darren Wilson had just broken. It was the thirteenth and the Ferguson uprising had been ongoing since the ninth. Black rage was roiling through the streets; Black grief was bringing folks to their knees, hands up.

If you can't recall the moment, perhaps you nonetheless know the image. Crawford's arc of movement became one of the most iconic images of Ferguson and Black Lives Matter—the moment, the movement. I know

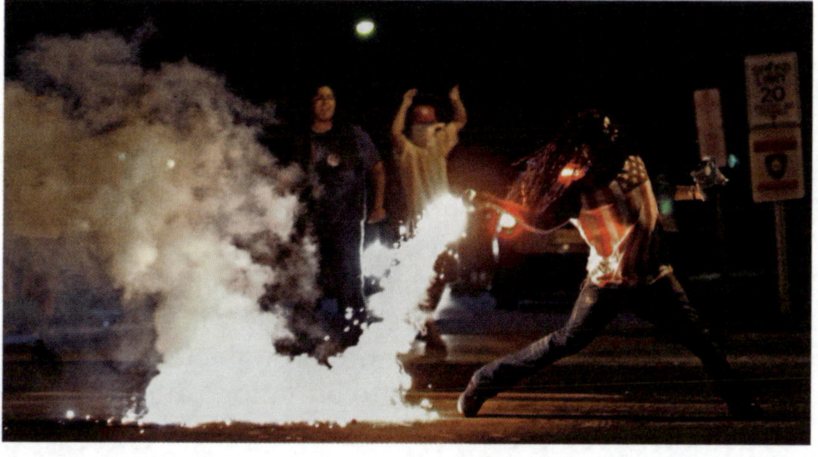

Edward Crawford returns a tear gas canister fired by police who were trying to disperse protesters in Ferguson, MO, on August 13, 2014. © Robert Cohen/ *St. Louis Post-Dispatch* via ZUMA Press Wire.

you remember it: Edward Crawford is wearing an American flag T-shirt and blue jeans, an open bag of chips in his hand. It's dark outside, but he's lit by the bright, searing light of a tear gas canister; the canister is on fire and trailing sulphureous, choking smoke. Crawford's locs fan out behind him, brushing across his face, nose, and mouth, as he throws the flaming canister away from protestors and back toward the militarized force occupying Ferguson.

Don't un-remember it now.

Two

Despite what many of us imagined our present moment would be, we are still in the midst of the pandemic in fall 2021. I imagine that we will be *here and now in the pandemic* for some time to come, and this is less unfortunate happenstance than a calculated risk on the part of the corporate-state governing apparatus. Rather than see an end to the pandemic itself, some have instead chosen to end the merely uncomfortable (for others, unimaginably painful) contortions their lives have taken. The results, of course, are everywhere: over four million dead worldwide, the toll still rising two years after the initial outbreak. In this way, the "post" in post-pandemic life becomes not a marker of the end but a marker of an ongoingness, an *aftermath*.

Aftermaths are the debris of catastrophe, collapse, and crisis. They are what remain, unwelcome and unwanted. What strikes me, again and again, are the ways aftermaths are accumulative: they are both an aggregate of and amplified by time. They are, like Karthik Pandian and Anthony Romero's "Five Theses Toward a Gathering of Big Brown," "in front of and behind, before and after."[1] *In frontness, behindness, beforeness, afterness*—these are precisely the aspects of aftermaths that escape, like sand through clenched fists. Despite their orientation to an "after," aftermaths insist upon preceding the very catastrophe, collapse,

1
See Anthony Romero and Karthik Pandian, "Five Theses toward a Gathering of Big Brown," in *Lastgaspism: Art and Survival in the Era of Pandemic*, 173.

AFTERMATH

and crisis they ostensibly follow. The aftermath is as much foresight as it is testimony. Is it any wonder that we must actively un-remember it?

Three

Since writing the end feels impossible, I will write the aftermath.

On May 4, 2017, mere years after the Ferguson uprising, Crawford was found dead. The St. Louis Metropolitan Police Department—centrally involved in efforts to quell the Ferguson protests—reported in the days following that Crawford had shot himself in the head. His death, as reported, was by suicide while riding in the backseat of a car with two other passengers.[2] Crawford's death hasn't been the only one worth a side eye—several other prominent Black Lives Matter activists have also died under suspicious circumstances.

Whether you believe Crawford's death to truly be a suicide or not, what remains is this: to be a Black person living in an anti-Black world compels a recognition of the ways Black death is never "natural" and rarely self-determined—not when death is preceded by a series of psychic, physical, and social traumas that compound. Entire nations are built upon the basis of this infrastructure.

Four

You may wonder why I write about a life and death several years past, instead of attending to the pandemic and the metaphorical, metaphysical, and material considerations of how we breathe in the now. Understand: I am compelled, simply and irreversibly, to attend to the long aftermath that even the pandemic—and how we breathe through it—is caught in. The mandate begins here: even in the face of a radically different every day, even in the face of a globally disquieting crisis, anti-Black violence continues. Without pause or hesitation.

2
Mary Emily O'Hara, "Ferguson Protester Edward Crawford, Subject of Iconic Photo, Found Dead," *NBC News*, May 5, 2017, https://www.nbcnews.com/news/us-news/ferguson-protester-edward-crawford-subject-iconic-photo-found-dead-n755401.

3

Christina Elizabeth Sharpe, *In the Wake: On Blackness and Being* (Durham, NC: Duke University Press, 2016).

4

Hunter Walker, "This Woman Was Maced inside the Capitol. She Told Me, 'It's a Revolution!,'" Twitter, January 6, 2021, https://twitter.com/hunterw/status/13469191715951 37025?s=20.

Christina Sharpe reminds us that we are ever in the wake of anti-Blackness.[3] Don't you un-remember this, now. I'm writing it all down for you.

Five

A tale of two cities: the first, Washington, DC, in the winter of 2021; the other, Philadelphia, Pennsylvania, in the summer of 2020.

On January 6, 2021, a horde of white supremacists rioted and staged an attempted coup. The mob—who were also Trump supporters—swarmed the US Capitol Building, terrorizing members of the House and Senate, Capitol Building staff, DC residents, and those of us who watched from afar. It was amid this chaos that Elizabeth from Knoxville, Tennessee, emerged. In what would quickly become a viral video, Elizabeth from Knoxville was interviewed as she left the scene of the coup. In the video, she can be seen gasping and grimacing, face twisted into a rictus of anguish as she struggles to speak, dabbing at her eyes with a blue towel (poorly concealing the weeping onion half clutched in its folds). As she tells it in the video: "I got maced . . . I made it like a foot inside [the Capitol Building] and they pushed me out and they *maced* me." To the interviewer's question, "And why did you wanna go in?," Elizabeth from Knoxville yells, overwrought, "We're storming the Capitol! It's a revolution!"[4]

To live under white supremacy is to know that white women have a long history of performing distress as a means of controlling and enacting violence against marginalized and racialized folks. Elizabeth from Knoxville conjured the mirage of hurt and harm, painting her white femaleness in it, and then, by identifying her home, Knoxville, Tennessee, she produced a mirage of a town filled with similarly injured, crying, overwrought white women who must leave their homes for the sake of the white supremacist revolution.

The aftermath: the *in frontness, behindness, beforeness, afterness.* Six months prior, on June 1, 2020,

Black Lives Matter protestors in Philadelphia, the city with the third largest Black population in the United States, were trapped on I-676 (the city's main highway).[5] This move was an intentional one by law enforcement, who proceeded to tear gas the protestors repeatedly, even though and especially because they were unable to escape. In the videos posted to Instagram and Twitter, protestors can be heard screaming, gasping out, "I can't breathe!" and yelling in confusion as they struggle—and fail—to scale a steep slope to escape the cloud of chemicals suffusing the air.[6]

5
Ellie Rushing, "Forever Changed," *Philadelphia Inquirer*, June 2, 2021, https://www.inquirer.com/news/philadelphia/a/protests-philadelphia-2020-676-teargas-police-20210602.html.

6
@Freerunsell, "June 1st, Philadelphia Police tear gassing peaceful protestors, trapped inside a fence in a highway. (Philadelphia, PA, 2020)," Instagram video, June 1, 2020, https://www.instagram.com/p/CA6R1eX A6uZ/. Image courtesy @Freerunsell.

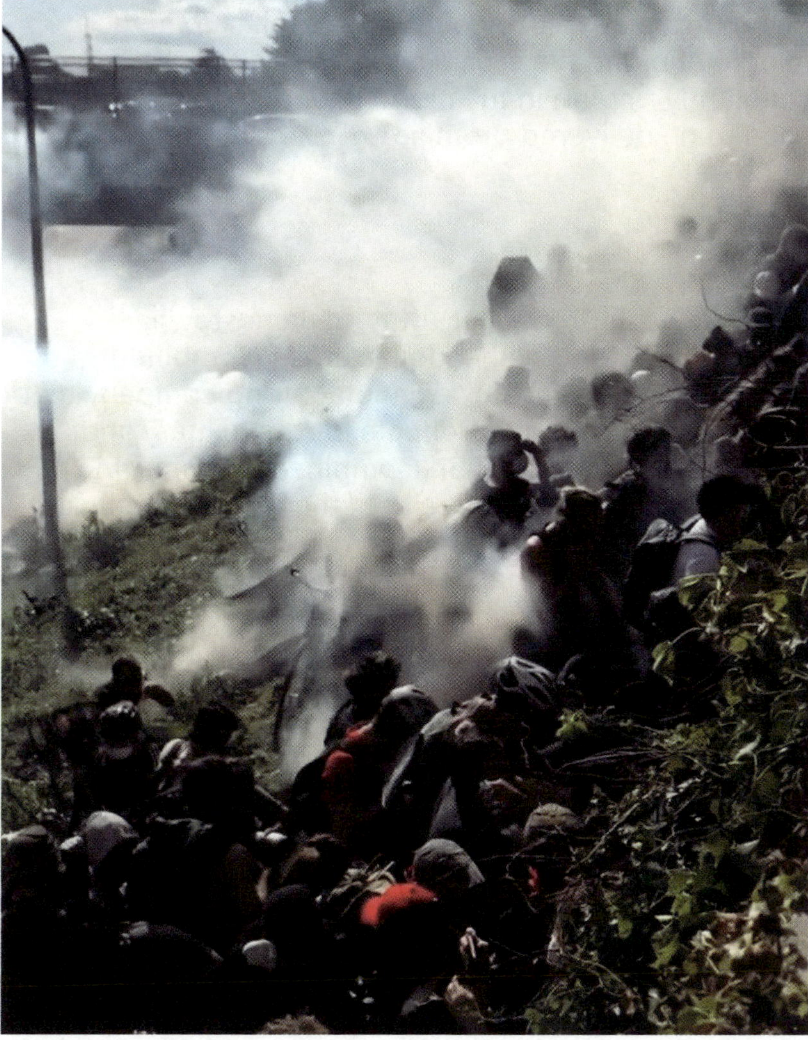

7 In 1985, the Philadelphia Police Department first tear gassed and then bombed a residential block in West Philadelphia, where members of MOVE resided. The bombing and resulting fire (which was left to burn by the Philadelphia Fire Department) killed eleven people (John Africa, Rhonda Africa, Theresa Africa, Frank Africa, Conrad Africa, Tree Africa, Delisha Africa, Netta Africa, Little Phil Africa, Tomaso Africa, and Raymond Africa). In April 2021, the *Philadelphia Inquirer* and the Billy Penn broke the news that the Penn Museum still held the remains of one of the children who died in the bombing. The remains were also, at one point, housed at Princeton University, where they were used as a "case study" in a Princeton course. For more on the MOVE bombing and its aftermath, see Teo Armus, "A Philly Museum Kept the Bones of a Black Child Killed in a Police Bombing. Decades Later, It's Apologizing," *Washington Post*, April 30, 2021, https://www.washingtonpost.com/nation/2 021/ 04/30/philadelphia-move- bomb-ing-bones-upenn/; Abdul-Aliy Muhammad, "Penn Museum Owes Reparations for Previously Holding Remains of a MOVE Bombing Victim," *Philadelphia Inquirer*, April 21, 2021, https://www.inquirer.com/opinion/commentary/penn-muse-um-reparations-repatria-tion-move-bombing-2021 0421.html; Maya Kassutto, "Remains of Children Killed in MOVE Bombing Sat in a Box at Penn Museum for Decades," Billy Penn

This wasn't the most egregious use of tear gas against Black Lives Matter protestors, nor was it the only act of terror committed by law enforcement and the vigilantes working alongside them. But in a city that remembers the MOVE bombing—a memory that still remains materially present in the buildings that have yet to be rebuilt and in the bodies that have been kept in the basements of the University of Pennsylvania and Princeton University—it was no coincidence that for *weeks* after the gassing, the Blackest parts of the city (in places like West Philly, especially areas west of the UPenn real estate chokehold) were plagued by loud, reverberating explosions that woke folks up in the middle of night, the *scat, scat, scat* of fireworks constantly ringing in the night air and the threat—the soon to be delivered promise—of tear gas in the home.[7]

Six

Only a few hundred miles away, in Jamestown, Pennsylvania, are the headquarters of Combined Tactical Systems (CTS), a manufacturing company that specializes in security products for the military and police. Also known as CSI (Combined Systems, Inc.), the company promotes itself as "the recognized leader in the design, manufacture, and marketing of security products for the global defense and law enforcement markets" and a "premier supplier of less-lethal munitions and launching systems," manufacturing products for "riot control, police tactical teams, corrections officers, and military units."[8] Its customer base includes "the U.S. Army, U.S. Marine Corps, U.S. Navy and a majority of the U.S. law enforcement, as well as foreign military and security forces around the world."[9] It is no stretch of the imagination to wonder whether CSI-branded tear gas was deployed at the Philadelphia protests. After all, the company received over $1.7 million in federal purchases in the first six months of 2020, in addition to providing munitions and training to law enforcement agencies across the country, despite a pandemic plaguing the nation.[10]

CSI's "less-lethal" munitions include defense aerosols "intended to cause varying degrees of pain and injury, which are temporary."[11] We know them by their colloquial term: tear gas. Tear gas is a catchall term for a host of chemical weapons that have been categorized as "less-lethal" and "riot-control" agents. Included in this category are concentrated pepper spray (oleoresin capsicum), CR (dibenzoxazepine), CN (chloroaceto-phenone), and CS (2-chlorobenzalmalononitrile). CSI's description of its less-lethal munitions continues: "These products . . . are used to gain compliance, disperse crowds, restore order, or temporarily incapacitate dangerous persons."[12] What could be more dangerous than a rebellion? And what better way to curtail a rebellion than by terrorizing the very air we breathe?

The deployment of tear gas at sites of anti-settler, anti-colonial, anti-racist struggle has become the tactic par excellence to force marches to disperse, cause avoidable deaths, and portray fleeing protestors as out-of-control rioters. Its use is so widespread that the effects of being sprayed with tear gas are well known by protestors globally: vomiting, crying, coughing, the inability to breathe, short-term blindness, and death. As Kristen Simmons writes, "humans 'simply cannot not breathe,' which is why atmospheric weapons are a profound form of terror(ism) that create atmospheres of apprehension."[13] Atmospheric weapons produce their own atmospheric infrastructures; we learn to navigate these infrastructures because they are real and material. Protest preparation, both in the US and elsewhere, has come to be shaped by the expectation of terror from the ground and from the air: folks do what they can to prepare for the fight for liberation with masks up, sunglasses, and full-coverage clothing like hoodies and jackets; with umbrellas and water bottles and towels; with traffic cones and chanting shouts; with an attention to their breath.

(website), April 21, 2021, https://billypenn.com/2021/04/21/move-bomb-ing-penn-museum-bones-remains-princeton-af-rica/?utm_source=dl vr. it&utm_medium=twitter.

8
"Who We Are," Combined Systems, accessed September 10, 2021, https://www.combinedsys-tems.com/.

9
"Who We Are."

10
Leticia Miranda, "Behind America's Tear Gas Business Boom: Low-Wage Workers and Angry Neighbors," *NBC News*, July 13, 2020, https://www.nbcnews.com/business/business-news/behind-america-s-tear-gas-busi-ness-boom-low-wage-work-ers-n1231729.

11
"MK-9 OC Vapor Products," Combined Systems, accessed September 10, 2021, https://www.combinedsystems.com/product/mk-9-oc-vapor-products/.

12
"MK-9 OC Vapor Products."

13
Kristen Simmons, "Settler Atmospherics," Society for Cultural Anthropology (website), November 20, 2017, https://culanth.org/fieldsights/settler-atmo-spherics.

Seven

I've often wondered what shadow infrastructures we would find if we traced the aftermath of the white supremacist state-sanctioned suppression of liberation struggles. I mean this on the metaphysical level, but also, most urgently, on the physical, material level. When the deployment of tear gas and other chemical compounds is a favored tactic by the United States military and law enforcement to suppress the freedom struggles of disenfranchised communities, and when communities are left to clean up the aftermath of these attacks, the presence of toxic particulate matter compounds until entire shadow cities grow in Black geographies.

During the 2014 Ferguson uprising, law enforcement tear gassed the residents of Ferguson with brutal and callous regularity. It's not an exercise in abstraction or speculation to know that the infrastructure of the built environment—the roads, the buildings, the very air—of Ferguson was forever changed after those nights of protest. What did Ferguson look like on a molecular level before the city and its predominantly Black residents were tear gassed, continuously for almost a month in 2014 and again in 2015 after Wilson wasn't indicted for his crimes?

Eight

The aftermath of the gassing of protestors on I-676, the aftermath of Ferguson: law enforcement unleashed further tear gas in the predominately Black neighborhood of West Philly. As the *Philadelphia Inquirer* reported after a month-long investigation, compiling interviews with community members and independent journalists, the deployment of tear gas in West Philly was primarily along residential streets, away from where protestors were marching and looting.[14] The smoke drifted inside people's homes—the only place they could have sheltered from the ongoing pandemic.

14
Aubrey Whelan et al., "Beseiged, Then Betrayed," *Philadelphia Inquirer*, July 17, 2020, https://www.inquirer.com/crime/a/west-philadelphia-52nd-street-protest-police-response-tear-gas-20200717.html.

Cleaning up tear gas inside a building is, as Aftermath (a company specializing in trauma cleaning and biohazard removal) explains, "extremely difficult and requires special equipment and trained technicians. Therefore, you should never attempt to remove tear gas on your own from the scene, and you should turn to a professional remediation company for help."[15] The chemical residue "can seep into porous materials like furniture, mattresses, clothing, carpet and even hardwood floors, and continue to irritate the mucous membranes of anyone residing in or visiting the property long after the incident."[16] *Furniture, mattresses, clothing, carpet*—these household objects hold the traces of violence in ways that can doubly violate flesh. It echoes the way property, and proper bookkeeping, mattered to the Victorian and antebellum homes that held persons in bondage. There, violence imposes itself upon Black flesh through an equative logic: both flesh and household object are "things" to be owned, sold and used. Cheryl Derricote's "Pandemic Bookkeeping" knows and names this aftermath.[17] In her images, all that is left are the icons of capitalism and modernity: the wine glasses, the champagne flutes, the serving bowls. We are left with a negative inventory—left to imagine the arms that set the table and the bodies sold to afford the champagne—of the things, living and dead, that an anti-Black world wants eradicated. All these things—living and dead—should not be seen, can no longer remain.

But, for a community rich with Black history: How many household things have faced deterioration or been lost as a result of chemical contamination? Kelli Morgan, in her interview with Daniel Tucker, notes that her passion for Black material culture came directly from her grandfather and the attic of wonders they shared: "[On] Sundays if it was raining or if my friends were gone at church, I would go into the attic. And I would pull out, I mean, just all kinds of stuff. I would sit there and just make up stories. . . . [I] remember that my grandfather would come up to the attic and give me the whole rundown about what was happening in the

15
"How to Remove Tear Gas in 7 Steps," Aftermath, accessed July 15, 2021, https://www.aftermath.com/content/how-to-remove-tear-gas/.

16
"How to Remove Tear Gas in 7 Steps."

17
See Cheryl Derricote, Pandemic Housekeeping, in *Lastgaspism*, 139.

18
Kelli Morgan quoted in Daniel Tucker, "Silence Won't Save You: Interview with Kelli Morgan," in *Lastgaspism*, 123.

19
Kenneth Bailey quoted in Anthony Romero, "An Ecology of Arrangements: An Interview with DS4SI," in *Lastgaspism*, 100.

country, why these objects were in the attic, what the familial story was as to whose objects they were."[18]

I quote that powerful moment at length because attics—a Black geography containing not only testimony but also insight—are spaces of holding out and hiding out. (You do remember Harriet Jacobs, don't you?) They are also, as Kenneth Bailey, one of the principals at the Design Studio for Social Intervention, states, examples of spaces "that can function as a kind of epistemological meeting ground, where ways of understanding the world can come together to render new ways of imagining the world."[19] And yet, these spaces rarely escape the violence that is tendered upon bodies. As tear gas seeps into Black homes and its residue renders everything toxic and outside the realm of saving, the very stories we tell and the grammars by which we can change the world are lost.

Nine

Do you remember the protest in Philly, your eyes burning, throat closing? Do you remember the hands that pulled you over the fence, pulled you away from the cops advancing on folks trying to flee? Do you remember, later, gentle hands helping you wash your eyes out with water, fire running down the back of your throat? Do you remember the gas? Do you remember the hands?

Do you?

Ten

I am writing the aftermath but not clearly enough. Let me try again.

In the aftermath, communities are left to clean up their homes and themselves, despite the fact that chemical weapons like tear gas have intense decontamination protocols. These are the steps one must take to

decontaminate themselves after encountering tear gas:
Hold your breath. Close your eyes. Get out of there.
Rinse your eyes. Wash your hands. Change your clothes.
Take a cold shower.[20]

Gasp.

Gasp.

Gasp.

I think, sometimes, about the urgent breath in Saul Williams's performance of "Ohm."[21] In it, he articulates the metaphysical infrastructures of breathing: the Black liberatory artistic tradition (beat boxing, slam poetry) alongside Hinduism. The plentiful beatboxing of the live performance becomes a rushing force, conjuring the practice of DJing, of standing before turntables and mixing universes for others to dance to, whip to, grind to, live to. Williams's "Ohm" *is* breath: the agitated and heaving gasps between the recital of each line, the sweat coating Williams's body as he exerts himself. Williams's breath control is impressive, each line delivered until his breath runs out, runs away, "towards the horizon of excess, toward becoming too much."[22]

What ecstasy, to self-determine the kinds of breathing and forms of gasping we practice.

Eleven

The question of infrastructure lingers for me, especially as we are caught in the rhythms of anti-Blackness, capitalist extraction, Indigenous dispossession, environmental ruin, colonial land grabbing and warfare, and so forth. This retrenchment is only possible through the malleability and ontogenesis of new infrastructures, many of which are invisible. Some of these infrastructures become foundational to *how* and *where* we seek liberation: Erin Genia rightly cautions against the tendency of "scholars, artists, leaders, scientists, and others operating within the Western cultural framework [to] expropriate" from Indigenous people's knowledges (in particular) and other cultures (more capaciously).[23] If we're to exist

20
"How to Remove Tear Gas in 7 Steps."

21
Paul Devlin (DevlinPix), "SlamNation - Saul Williams - 'Ohm,'" YouTube, September 30, 2010, https://www.youtube.com/watch?v=KJHquOEChRg.

22
Devlin, "SlamNation - Saul Willams - 'Ohm.'"

23
See Erin Genia, "Breaking Down to Build Up: A Cultural Emergency Response," in *Lastgaspism*, 76.

24
Dan S. Wang, "Enlighten-
ment of Color," in
Lastgaspism, 153.

25
Damon Locks, "Then X
Enters," in *Lastgaspism*, 115.

outside the metaphysical infrastructures of the West, where do we begin without replicating harm? Is there a way to attend to the necessary cross-pollination of practices and traditions, the way Dan S. Wang explores in "Enlightenment of Color" via the blossoming of Buddhist meditation and chanting across racialized communities, liberation fighters, and abolitionists?[24]

When folks are turning to varied metaphysical practices of breathing to attend to their liberatory practices, I am reminded—again—that liberation is unnavigable on the individual level.

Twelve

Damon Locks's "Then X Enters" is where I must go: "Is there a light in a dark city called Liberation?"[25] The aftermaths of this kind of "atmoterror"—not only tear gas in the streets as we protest and inside our homes in the midst of a pandemic, but also the intense, sticky, and broiling summer air inside prisons that house predominantly Black and brown bodies, leading to incarcerated folks suffering from heat stroke and death; the forest fires plaguing California and filling the air with soot, an event first experienced by Los Angeles' Black and brown communities living along the city's highway system; the way many Black folks were deemed "essential workers" in the pandemic and expected to be at higher risk of exposure to COVID-19 so that the nation's fiscal health could be maintained; and so many, many more—against Black folks are not and cannot be solely violent ones. As Williams's "Ohm" reminds me, gasping (whether it is our first or our last) can be ecstasy. It can be refusal. It can be care, like the hands that usher us to safety when we are gasping from tear gas.

Is it any wonder that *care*, as Daniel Tucker directs our attention to in his piece "Care in Crisis," has remained foundational to the language of coalition? As Tucker writes: "'Care' was also already on the tongues of a growing number of social theorists, artists, and community organizers alike in the language connecting the struggles."[26] Alchemizing noun into verb, Tucker takes us through tender and painful artists' engagements with care, care work, care-fullness, community care, and caring. As Tucker moves from site to site, mission to mission, radical commitment to radical commitment, we move with him, carefully guided to places we can't see.

Thirteenth

In the early days of the pandemic, every time I walked past a discarded, rumpled mask on the sidewalk I remember thinking: *How can folks lose their masks—the thing meant to allow them to* breathe*—in a pandemic?* My question could do nothing but transmutate when taken to the tender insides of our lungs with the overexposure of Pato Hebert's Lingering series: How do we handle catastrophic loss—of people, of movements, of breath?[27]

An *after all this*—if *this* means the infrastructures of disenfranchisement and violation that have propped up our current world schema for centuries—won't exist until we end this world. Genia had the phrasing right: break down to build up—not with the same materials, but new ones. Not with the same tools, but different ones. An end to all this won't come until we end all this: this is what a commitment to abolition means. As Sandra de la Loza reminds us: "The tools of sitting, breathing, and listening are parallel with the tools of a paintbrush, of printmaking, or a camera, or a guitar, or our bodies in dance, or whatever creative tools we may use."[28]

The *aftermath* is the *longue durée* of the everyday catastrophe. In it, we find the traces and remnants of things that seem impossible to lose, and yet we do. But we also sometimes find new networks between people who care. In the spaces between, we hold on to what might be forgotten.

I've been writing it all down. This is my tool for dreaming a different aftermath, sifting through the

26
See Daniel Tucker, "Care in Crisis," in *Lastgaspism*, 53.

27
Pato Hebert, "Asynchronous Lingering and the Capillaries of Care," in *Lastgaspism*, 35.

28
Sandra de la Loza quoted in Dan S. Wang, "Exhaling Peace," in *Lastgaspism*, 33.

remnants of the dreams we needed, wanted, and couldn't manifest.

Since writing the end feels impossible, I will write the aftermath of our next and our current pandemic.

It was August 13, 2014. Don't un-remember it again now.

KENNETH BAILEY is the cofounder of the Design Studio for Social Intervention (DS4SI). His interests focus on the research and development of design tools for marginalized communities to address complex social issues. With over three decades of experience in community practice, Bailey brings a unique perspective on the ethics of design in relation to community engagement, the arts, and cultural action. Projects he has coproduced at DS4SI include Action Lab (2012–present), Public Kitchen (2011–present), Social Emergency Response Center (2017–present), and the People's Redevelopment Authority (2018). Bailey was recently a visiting scholar in collaboration with the University of Tasmania and also a founding member of Theatrum Mundi NYC with Richard Sennett. His new book (coauthored with DS4SI) is entitled *Ideas—Arrangements—Effects: Systems Design and Social Justice* (Minor Compositions, 2020). He has an MFA from Bennington College.

KIMBERLY BAIN thinks, writes, teaches, and speaks on Blackness from the 19th century to the contemporary moment. In her scholarly and critical-creative work, her most pressing and urgent concerns have consolidated around questions of the history, theory, and philosophy of Blackness. She is currently at work on two book projects. The first, *On Black Breath*, takes the charge of "I can't breathe" and considers breath as more than the mere metaphor—but rather as also a sociopolitical phenomenon. Her second book project, *Dirt: Soil and Other Dark Matters*, turns to dirt for understanding how Blackness has shaped global considerations of the Anthropocene and refused the extractive relations of racial capitalism.

SANDRA DE LA LOZA is a Los Angeles artist whose research-based practice includes walks, field investigations, visits to archives, and participation in local community struggles. She investigates the underlying power dynamics embedded in social space while exposing the gaps, absences, and the in-between spaces within dominant historical narratives through performative, social, and aesthetic strategies that result in multimedia installations, video, photography, social engagement, and public interventions. Her recent work scrutinizes the underlayers of our present landscape as a means to decolonize and heal ancestral trauma, and to create circles that enable other social relations to happen. Recent exhibits include *Undoing Time: Histories of Art and Incarceration* (Arizona State University Art Museum, 2021–22), *Talking to Action: Art, Activism, Pedagogy of the Americas* (Valparaiso, Chile, 2021), and *Imagining De-Gentrified* (APEX Art, New York, 2020).

CHERYL DERRICOTTE is a visual artist, and her favorite mediums are glass and paper. Originally from Washington, DC, she lives and works in San Francisco, CA. Her art has been featured in numerous publications, including the *New York Times*, the *Guardian*, and the *San Francisco Chronicle*. She has been an artist-in-residence at Villa San Francisco and Paper Machine New Orleans; a Windgate Craft Fellow at Vermont Studio Center; a Hemera Foundation Tending Space Artist Fellow; an inaugural emerging artist at the Museum of the African Diaspora; and a 2020 YBCA100 listee. She holds a BA in Urban Affairs from Barnard College; an MRP from Cornell University; and an MFA from the California Institute of Integral Studies. In 2021, she was awarded the commission to develop a monument to Harriet Tubman at the new BART transit-oriented development, Gateway at Millbrae Station; it is believed that it will be the first sculptural tribute to Tubman in glass.

ERIN GENIA (Sisseton-Wahpeton Dakota) is a multidisciplinary artist, educator, and organizer whose practice merges cultural imperatives, pure expression, and material exploration with the conceptual to amplify the powerful presence of Indigeneity on the occupied lands of the US and in the arts, sciences, and public realm. Genia has an MS in Art, Culture, and Technology from Massachusetts Institute of Technology and has recently exhibited her work at the Venice Biennale, Ars Electronica, and the International Space Station. Genia served as a 2020 artist in residence for the City of Boston and worked with the New England Foundation for the Arts public art team on the project *Centering Justice: Indigenous Artists' Perspectives on Public Art.*

PATO HEBERT is an artist, teacher, and organizer. His creative projects have appeared at Beton7 in Athens, the Centro de Arte Contemporáneo in Quito, the Ballarat International Foto Biennale, and IHLIA LGBT Heritage in Amsterdam. He is as an associate arts professor and serves as chair in the Department of Art & Public Policy at the Tisch School of the Arts at New York University. Since 1994 he has worked with social movements and community organizations to develop innovative approaches to HIV mobilization, programs, advocacy, and justice. He is a COVID-19 long hauler, living with the impacts of the coronavirus and publicly addressing the pandemic since March 2020.

LORI LOBENSTINE is the program design lead and cofounder of the Design Studio for Social Intervention (DS4SI). At DS4SI she has helped design and lead such interventions as Public Kitchen and Social Emergency Response Center (SERC), as well as civic engagement projects including GoBoston 2030, Upham's Corner Arts & Innovation District, and the speculative People's Redevelopment Authority. Her consulting practice includes national facilitation work around diversity, equity, and design in the fields of public health, education, and urban planning. Her writings include "Spatial Justice: A Frame for Reclaiming Our Rights to Be, Thrive, Express and Connect" (available at http://ds4si.org) and DS4SI's new book *Ideas—Arrangements—Effects: Systems Design and Social Justice* (Minor Compositions, 2020).

DAMON LOCKS is a Chicago-based visual artist, educator, and vocalist/musician. He is a Museum of Contemporary Art/SPACE (School Partnership for Art and Civic Engagement) embedded artist at Sarah E. Goode STEM Academy. He teaches art with Prison + Neighborhood Arts Project at Statesville Correctional Center. He is a recipient of the Helen Coburn Meier and Tim Meier Achievement Award in the Arts, a 3Arts awardee, and a Soros Justice Media Fellow. Locks leads the musical group Black Monument Ensemble and is a founding member of The Eternals. He is also the primary vocalist in Rob Mazurek's Exploding Star Orchestra.

DR. KELLI MORGAN is professor of the practice and director of curatorial studies at Tufts University. A respected scholar, curator, educator, and social justice activist, her scholarly commitment to the investigation of anti-Blackness within American art and visual culture has demonstrated how traditional art history and museum practices uphold white supremacy. Besides her own curatorial experience, she mentors emerging curators and regularly trains staff at various museums to foster anti-racist approaches in collection-building, exhibitions, community engagement, and fundraising. In 2020–21, Morgan became a leading public voice in bolstering anti-racist work at art museums.

KARTHIK PANDIAN is an artist who works in exhibitions and public interventions to unsettle the ground of history. Pandian has had solo exhibitions at the Whitney Museum of American Art; Bétonsalon, Paris; and Midway Contemporary Art, Minneapolis, amongst others. His work has been featured in numerous international survey exhibitions, including the inaugural Hammer Museum LA Biennial; Okwui Enwezor's *La Triennale: Intense Proximity*, Palais de Tokyo, Paris; and *Adventures of the Black Square: Abstract Art and Society 1915-2015*, Whitechapel Gallery, London. In 2019, he presented *Atlas Unlimited*, a collaboration with choreographer Andros Zins-Browne, sculptor Zakaria Almoutlak, and many others, at 80 Washington Square East in New York City. He is currently working on temporary public artworks for Boston and Minneapolis and a series of movement workshops animated by Diego Rivera's Detroit Industry Murals. Pandian received his BA in Art Semiotics and Comparative Literature from Brown University and his MFA from Art Center College of Design. He teaches in the Department of Art, Film, and Visual Studies at Harvard University.

ANTHONY ROMERO is a Boston-based artist, writer, and organizer committed to documenting and supporting artists and communities of color. Recent projects and performances have been featured at the Bemis Center for Contemporary Arts (Omaha), the Blue Star Contemporary (San Antonio), the Institute of Contemporary Art (Boston) and the Mountain Standard Time Performative Art Biennial (Calgary, Canada). Publications include *The Social Practice that Is Race*, coauthored with Dan S. Wang, and the exhibition catalogue *Organize Your Own: The Politics and Poetics of Self-Determination Movements*, which he edited. He was a 2019–20 fellow at the Radcliffe Institute for Advanced Study at Harvard University.

DANIEL TUCKER works as an educator, artist, writer, and organizer developing documentaries, publications, exhibitions, and events inspired by his interest in social movements and the people and places from which they emerge. His recent projects include *Power Map* with Mural Arts Philadelphia and *Confronting Enemies* with A Blade of Grass (New York). His writings and lectures on the intersections of art and politics and his collaborative art projects have been published and presented widely, and are documented on the archive miscprojects.com. He is currently an assistant professor and the founding graduate program director in socially engaged art at Moore College of Art & Design in Philadelphia.

DAN S. WANG is an artist currently living in Los Angeles. He was a founding keyholder of Mess Hall, an experimental cultural space in Chicago, and currently works in the collaborative vehicle Now-Time Asian America. Recent projects include commissioned works for the Station Museum (Houston) and Asian Arts Initiative (Philadelphia). He exhibited *A Ragbox of Overstood Grammars*, a retrospective of eighty-plus letterpress prints at Fonderie Darling (Montreal) in 2020. His art writings have been published internationally in book collections, museum catalogues, and dozens of artist publications. He is an artist in residence at 18th Street Arts Center in Santa Monica. He holds an undergraduate degree in religion.

p. 43–51   All images by Pato Hebert: *Untitled*, Lingering series, 2020–21. Digital photographs. Courtesy of the artist.

p. 74   Erin Genia, *InVisible*, 2017. Pieced organza and shawl fringe, 60 × 60 inches. Image: Zacharia Jamaria and Gary Zhexi Zhang.

p. 78   Erin Genia, *Cultural Emergency Response*, 2020–21. Digital graphic. Courtesy of the artist.

p. 82   Erin Genia, *Deeply Embedded Detrimental Tenets Mindmap*, 2021. Infographic. Courtesy of the artist.

p. 86   Erin Genia, *Facing/Not Facing: Toxic Devastation from Oil*, 2016. Glazed terracotta, brass, plaster, wood, acrylic; 18 × 12 × 3 inches. Courtesy of the artist.

p. 90   Erin Genia, *Colonial Legacy: Uncontrolled Burn*, 2018. Pastel on paper, 16 × 20 inches. Courtesy of the artist.

p. 94   Erin Genia, *Iȟpéya/Piyéhpičašni: Midnight Mine Goblet*, 2018. Glazed ceramic, 8 × 7 × 6 inches. Courtesy of the artist.

p. 114   Damon Locks, *A Lost Place (pg. 1)*, 2020. Ink on paper, 12 × 9.75 in. Photo: Ryan Edmund. Courtesy of Goldfinch Gallery, Chicago, IL.

Soberscove Press
Chicago, Illinois
soberscove.com

*Lastgaspism: Art and Survival
in The Age of Pandemic* © 2022
Soberscove Press
All artwork © the artists
All texts © the authors

All rights reserved. No part of this publication may be reproduced, stored in retrieval systems, or transmitted in any form or by any means, electronic, mechanical, photocopying, recording or otherwise, without the prior permission of the copyright holder.

ISBN 978-1-940190-31-0
Design: Dorothy Lin
Printed in Lithuania

Distributed by
ARTBOOK | D.A.P.
75 Broad Street, Suite 630
New York, NY 10004
artbook.com

The authors would like to thank their families for their support during this challenging time in which to work and live. They would also like to extend their thanks to all of the contributors, designer Dorothy Lin, and especially publisher Julia Klein for their deep engagement and collaboration over the last year. The process of making this book with such a committed team was a bright light in anxious times.

Library of Congress Cataloging-in-Publication Data

Names: Romero, Anthony. | Tucker, Daniel, 1983- | Wang, Daniel S.
Title: Lastgaspism : art and survival in the age of pandemic / by Anthony Romero, Daniel Tucker, Dan S. Wang ; with Kimberly Bain, Sandra de la Loza, Cheryl Derricotte, Design Studio for Social Intervention, Erin Genia, Pato Hebert, Damon Locks, Kelli Morgan, Karthik Pandian.
Description: Chicago, Illinois : Soberscove Press, [2022] | Includes bibliographical references.
Identifiers: LCCN 2021049132 | ISBN 9781940190310 (paperback)
Subjects: LCSH: Art and society--United States--History--21st century. | COVID-19 Pandemic, 2020-
Classification: LCC N72.S6 L374 2022 | DDC 701/.03--dc23/ eng/20211027 LC record available at https://lccn.loc. gov/2021049132

Cover Image: Pato Hebert, *Untitled*, Lingering series, 2020–21. Digital photograph. Courtesy of the artist.

200